D0840281

The Insiders

by

JOHN F. MCMANUS

The John Birch Society
Appleton, Wisconsin 54913-8040

Fourth edition, first printing, February 1995 .... 25,000 copies

Published by
The John Birch Society
Post Office Box 8040
Appleton, Wisconsin 54913
414–749–3780

Printed in the United States of America
Library of Congress Catalog Card Number: 92–73378
ISBN: 1–881919–02–1

Contents

Contents

About the Author

John F. McManus joined the staff of The John Birch Society as a Field Coordinator in New England in 1966. He earned promotion to the headquarters staff in 1968. In 1973, he was appointed Public Relations Director and worked very closely with the Society's founder, Robert Welch (1899-1985).

In conjunction with his public relations duties, Mr. McManus became the organization's chief spokesman. He has appeared on many hundreds of radio and television programs, and has given an equal number of interviews to members of the press. He has travelled the nation extensively and has conducted Society business in every one of the 50 states.

A native of Brooklyn, New York, Mr. McManus earned a Bachelor of Science degree from Holy Cross College in Massachusetts, served for three years as a Marine Corps officer, and was employed for six years in the early 1960s as an electronics engineer. Married in 1957, he and his wife are the parents of four.

He is a writer, film and television producer, editor, speaker, and newspaper columnist. His *Birch Log* columns have provided valuable insight about the affairs of our nation since 1973. His book *An Overview Of Our World* (1971) analyzed the great conspiracy against mankind. His *Financial Terrorism: Hijacking America Under the Threat of Bankruptcy* (1993) supplies valuable insights about national debt, federal deficits, inflation, and the Federal Reserve.

In 1989, Mr. McManus accepted appointment as Publisher of *The New American* magazine, and in 1991, he was named President of The John Birch Society.

Preface

In addition to previously published surveys of Insider domination of the administrations of Jimmy Carter, Ronald Reagan, and George Bush, this edition of *The Insiders* presents a new Part IV containing a survey of the control exercised by Insiders over the administration headed by Bill Clinton.

An important key to understanding the dominance of the Insiders over contemporary America begins with an understanding of the history and purposes of such organizations as the Council on Foreign Relations and the Trilateral Commission. Much of this history appears in Part I and is not repeated in Parts II, III, and IV. The definition of the term Insiders, as it was first given by John Birch Society founder Robert Welch, and as it has been employed by the Society ever since, is provided toward the end of Part I.

Readers familiar with the author's critiques of the Carter, Reagan and Bush administrations are encouraged to turn immediately to Part IV, the survey of the beginning years of the Clinton administration. Others who are new to the kind of analysis given here would do well to skip nothing because the national agenda has been set by Insiders during all of these years. The pattern of Insider dominance over America's affairs is itself an important part of the story told in this book.

We hope that this glimpse of the increasing Insider control over the U.S. government and other critically important areas of American life will stimulate many to become involved in the fight to turn the Insiders out.

Each portion of this book closes with an invitation to all to join The John Birch Society. We repeat that earnestly given invitation here as we present the fourth edition of this painstakingly researched book.

THE JOHN BIRCH SOCIETY
February 1995

Introduction

If a member of your family were suddenly felled by a strange malady, you would quickly run to the family physician. So, too, would you hasten to a doctor's office when a more familiar disease struck, or when an accident caused a broken bone or torn flesh.

Once in the presence of the doctor, you would hardly waste his time or your own by demanding of him some assurance that he favors good health. You know he already does. And you know he opposes fever, earaches, broken legs, etc.

We mention this because The John Birch Society has often been accused of promoting only negativism, or of merely finding fault. Yet any honest survey of our literature demonstrates that such a charge is baseless. The doctor who wants healthy bodies doesn't take time to explain that he wants good health. Nor do we always explain that our first and foremost goal is a strong nation and a healthy civilization.

The Insiders explains much of what has gone wrong in America and who is causing her ills. We doubt that we will be accused of presuming too greatly in believing that most Americans know something is eating away at the foundations of this great nation. Unemployment, national and personal indebtedness, economic slowdown, loss of faith, declining national stature, a vaguely defined "new world order," broken families, and much more have stimulated worries from coast to coast and from all sectors of our social and economic strata.

The John Birch Society believes in America — in her magnificent Constitution, her glorious traditions, and her wonderful people. Where America is strong, we seek to preserve; where she has been weakened, we seek to rebuild. Sadly, we witness the presence of powerful forces working to destroy the marvelous foundations given us by farseeing and noble men 200 years ago.

The information and analysis given in this book will undoubtedly upset, even anger, some readers. But if the history contained in these pages is disturbing to both the reader and ourselves, we urge that the blame be directed toward those who made it, not those who published it.

Doctors can't treat patients until they identify the causes of ailments. Similarly, no citizen can act to help his nation until he or she understands what constitutes good national health and what is ravishing it. It is our hope that the information presented in these pages will assist a great many more Americans to identify our nation's diseases — and those who spread them — and then take action to speed her back to the robust health she once enjoyed.

The Insiders

The Insiders
Part I — 1979

Immediately after World War II, the American people were subjected to a massive propaganda barrage which favored the Chinese communists and frowned on the Chinese Nationalists. Newspapers, books, magazines, and experts in government did their best to convince Americans that the Red Chinese were not communists at all, but were merely "agrarian reformers" seeking fair play for the Chinese people.[1]

In the midst of this propaganda blitz, our government completely turned its back on the Nationalist Chinese in 1947, refusing even to sell them arms. By 1949, the communist forces under Mao Tse-tung had seized all of mainland China. After the communist takeover, serious students of the situation lost no time in declaring that China had been lost in Washington, not in Peking or Shanghai. And they were correct.[2]

Eventually, the full truth about the Chinese communists became widely known. A U.S. Senate subcommittee report,[3] published in 1971, contains gruesome statistics which show that the Chinese communists have murdered as many as 64 million of their countrymen. Despite current propaganda to the contrary, Communist China continues to this day to be one of the most brutal tyrannies in the history of mankind. And the Chinese Reds have exported revolution and terror to every continent.

The American people were misled thirty years ago. If the truth about China had been widely

1

known, our government would never have intervened in the Chinese struggle as it did. China would not have fallen into communist hands; there would never have been a Korean War in the 1950s; and there would never have been a Vietnam War in the 1960s and 70s. The course of history would have taken a far different path — if only the American people had not been misled about the Chinese communists.

In the late 1950s, the American people were again misled. We were told that Fidel Castro was the "Robin Hood of the Sierra Maestra Mountains," and that he was the "George Washington of Cuba." Some Americans knew better and tried to spread the alarm. But, in spite of their efforts, our government repeated the process it had followed in China and Castro eventually seized control of Cuba.[4]

Again, the American people had been misled. If the truth about Castro had been widely known, our press and our government would never have aided him, and he would never have succeeded in capturing Cuba and in spreading communist subversion throughout Latin America — and now even into Africa.

The question we must ask ourselves today is: Are there any other important but similarly erroneous attitudes that have been planted in the minds of the American people? The answer is that there certainly are.

One dangerously wrong attitude held by many Americans is that all prominent businessmen in America — the American capitalists as they are called — are by definition the archenemies of communism.

In fact, the mere suggestion that a prominent

capitalist, like David Rockefeller, is in league with communists invites scorn or ridicule. The notion appears to many to be totally absurd because a man like David Rockefeller, it seems, would have so much to lose if the communists should ever triumph.

But, in the last few years, David Rockefeller's Chase Manhattan Bank has been favored by the Reds as the first American bank to open an office in Moscow, and also the first to do so in Peking. And this same Chase Manhattan Bank has bankrolled the building of the largest truck factory in the history of mankind, at a place called the Kama River in the Soviet Union. It is totally inaccurate to consider David Rockefeller an enemy of communism.

It is also inaccurate to believe that all prominent businessmen in our nation are conservatives who are always the most determined opponents of socialistic government controls. We agree that businessmen should be anti-communists, and that they should be advocates of limited government, as given us by our Founding Fathers. But many are not.

As communism continues to advance toward total world domination, as America's place in the world slips from undisputed leadership to second-rate status, and as our own federal government's control over all of us grows with each passing day, many Americans are looking for an explanation of what they see happening.

We believe that the first step toward learning what is really going on in our country is the realization that some so-called capitalists are neither conservative nor anti-communist. Instead, they are power-seekers who are using their great wealth and influence to achieve political control. What follows will take a hard look at what we perceive as an ongoing drive for power. Not only the kind of power that flows from great wealth, but absolute power, the kind that can only be achieved politically. We are going to take a look behind the headlines at the men who really run our country, the men whom Jimmy Carter called "the insiders."

Who Is Running America?

One of President Jimmy Carter's favorite themes during his campaign for the Presidency in 1976 was that, if he were elected, he would bring new faces and new ideas to Washington. He repeatedly told campaign audiences that he was not part of the federal government and not beholden to the Washington-and-New York-based Establishment that had been running things for so long.

Perhaps the clearest example of his campaign oratory against what he called the Insiders was given at a Carter-for-President Rally in Boston on February 17, 1976. What he said on that occasion showed up in a widely distributed paperback *'I'll Never Lie To You' — Jimmy Carter In His Own Words*.[5] On page 48, Mr. Carter's statement at that Boston Rally is given as follows:

> The people of this country know from bitter experience that we are not going to get these changes merely by shifting around the same groups of insiders.... The insiders have had their chance and they have not delivered.

The message undoubtedly persuaded a good

many Americans to cast their ballots for Jimmy Carter, for the existence of such an inside group running things is both widely suspected and widely resented. And yet, while the former governor of Georgia played up to this resentment throughout the campaign, he carefully avoided naming any names or discussing any of the organizational ties of the easily identifiable Insiders.

This, we intend to do. For we agree with Mr. Carter's campaign oratory that, for several decades, America has been run by a group of Establishment Insiders. We also intend to show that, despite his strong pledge to the contrary, Jimmy Carter has literally filled his administration with these same individuals. Since Jimmy Carter moved into Washington, it has been business as usual for the Insiders who are running the United States.

The man popularly credited with devising the strategy that landed Jimmy Carter in the White House is Hamilton Jordan. A few weeks prior to the November 1976 election, he stated:

> If, after the inauguration, you find a Cy Vance as Secretary of State and Zbigniew Brzezinski as head of National Security, then I would say we failed. And I would quit. You're going to see new faces and new ideas.[6]

After the election, Mr. Carter promptly named Cyrus Vance to be his Secretary of State and Zbigniew Brzezinski to be the head of National Security, exactly what Mr. Jordan had said would never happen. But the real question is: What is it about Mr. Vance and Mr. Brzezinski that prompted Jordan to make such a statement? And the answer is that these two men are pillars of the very Establishment that candidate Carter so often attacked.

When Jimmy Carter appointed him to be Secretary of State, Cyrus Vance was a Wall Street lawyer, the chairman of the board of the Rockefeller Foundation, and a veteran of service in the Kennedy, Johnson and Nixon administrations.

Zbigniew Brzezinski had taught at Harvard and Columbia Universities, served in the State Department during the Johnson administration, and authored numerous books and articles for various Establishment publishers and periodicals.

But, beyond all of these Establishment credentials, at the time of their appointment by Jimmy Carter, both Vance and Brzezinski were members of the board of directors of a little-known organization called the Council on Foreign Relations. Also, each was a member of the very exclusive Trilateral Commission. Most Americans have never heard of these two organizations. But knowing something about them is essential to understanding what has been going on in America for several decades. So, let us examine, first, the Council on Foreign Relations and then, later on, the Trilateral Commission.

The House Blueprint

The Council on Foreign Relations[7] was incorporated in 1921. It is a private group which is headquartered at the corner of Park Avenue and 68th Street in New York City, in a building given to the organization in 1929.

The CFR's founder, Edward Mandell House, had been the chief adviser of President Woodrow Wilson. House was not only Wilson's most prominent aide, he actually dominated the President. Woodrow Wilson referred to House as "my alter ego" (my other self), and it is totally accurate to say that House, not Wilson, was the most powerful individual in our nation during the Wilson administration, from 1913 until 1921.

Unfortunately for America, it is also true that Edward Mandell House was a Marxist whose goal was to socialize the United States. In 1912, House wrote the book, *Philip Dru: Administrator*.[8] In it, he said he was working for "Socialism as dreamed of by Karl Marx." The original edition of the book did not name House as its author, but he made it clear in numerous ways that he indeed was its creator.

In *Philip Dru: Administrator*, Edward Mandell House laid out a fictionalized plan for the conquest of America. He told of a "conspiracy" (the word is his) which would gain control of both the Democratic and Republican parties, and use them as instruments in the creation of a socialistic world government.

The book called for passage of a graduated income tax and for the establishment of a state-controlled central bank as steps toward the ultimate goal. Both of these proposals are planks in *The Communist Manifesto*.[9] And both became law in 1913, during the very first year of the House-dominated Wilson administration.

The House plan called for the United States to give up its sovereignty to the League of Nations at the close of World War I. But when the U.S. Senate refused to ratify America's entry into the League, Edward Mandell House's drive toward world government was slowed down. Disappointed, but not beaten, House and his friends then formed the Council on Foreign Relations, whose purpose right from its inception was to destroy the freedom and independence of the United States and lead our nation into a world government — if not through the League of Nations, then through another world organization that would be started after another world war. The control of that world government, of course, was to be in the hands of House and like-minded individuals.

From its beginning in 1921, the CFR began to attract men of power and influence. In the late 1920s, important financing for the CFR came from the Rockefeller Foundation and the Carnegie Foundation. In 1940, at the invitation of President Roosevelt, members of the CFR gained domination over the State Department, and they have maintained that domination ever since.

The Making of Presidents

By 1944, Edward Mandell House was deceased, but his plan for taking control of our nation's major political parties began to be realized. In 1944 and in 1948, the Republican candidate for President, Thomas Dewey, was a CFR member. In later years, the CFR could boast that Republicans Eisenhower and Nixon were members, as were Democrats Stevenson, Kennedy, Humphrey, and McGovern. The American people were told they had a choice when they voted for President. But with precious few exceptions, presidential candidates for decades have been CFR members.

But the CFR's influence had also spread to other vital areas of American life. Its members have run, or are running, NBC and CBS, the *New York Times*, the *Washington Post*, the *Des Moines*

Register, and many other important newspapers. The leaders of *Time, Life, Newsweek, Fortune, Business Week*, and numerous other publications are CFR members. The organization's members also dominate the academic world, top corporations, the huge tax-exempt foundations, labor unions, the military, and just about every segment of American life.[10]

Let's look at the Council's *Annual Report* published in 1978. The organization's membership list names 1,878 members, and the list reads like a *Who's Who in America*. Eleven CFR members are U.S. senators;[11] even more congressmen belong to the organization. Sitting on top of this immensely powerful pyramid, as chairman of the board, is David Rockefeller.

As can be seen in that CFR *Annual Report*, 284 of its members are U.S. government officials. Any organization which can boast that 284 of its members are U.S. government officials should be well-known. Yet most Americans have never even heard of the Council on Foreign Relations.

One reason why this is so is that 171 journalists, correspondents and communications executives are also CFR members, and they don't write about the organization. In fact, CFR members rarely talk about the organization inasmuch as it is an express condition of membership that any disclosure of what goes on at CFR meetings shall be regarded as grounds for termination of membership.[12]

Carter and CFR Clout

And so, very few Americans knew that something was wrong when Jimmy Carter packed his administration with the same crowd that has been running things for decades. When he won the Democratic Party's nomination, Jimmy Carter chose CFR member Walter Mondale to be his running mate. After the election, Mr. Carter chose CFR members Cyrus Vance, Harold Brown, and W. Michael Blumenthal to be the Secretaries of State, Defense and Treasury — the top three cabinet positions.

Other top Carter appointees who are CFR members include Joseph Califano, Secretary of HEW; Patricia Roberts Harris, Secretary of HUD; Stansfield Turner, CIA Director; Zbigniew Brzezinski, National Security Advisor; and Andrew Young, Ambassador to the United Nations. The names of scores of Assistant Secretaries, Undersecretaries, Ambassadors and other appointees can also be found on the CFR membership roster. As we have already noted, a total of 284 CFR members hold positions in the Carter administration.

To put it mildly, the Council on Foreign Relations has a great deal of clout. In our opinion, however, not every member of the CFR is fully committed to carrying out Edward Mandell House's conspiratorial plan. Many have been flattered by an invitation to join a study group, which is what the CFR calls itself. Others go along because of personal benefits such as a nice job and a new importance. But all are used to promote the destruction of U.S. sovereignty. Over the years, only a few members have ever had the courage and the awareness to speak out about the Council on Foreign Relations. These few are now ex-members who have always been ignored by the press.[13]

Toward World Government

The CFR publishes a very informative quarterly journal called *Foreign Affairs*. More often than not, important new shifts in U.S. policy or highly indicative attitudes of political figures have been telegraphed in its pages. When he was preparing to run for the Presidency in 1967, for instance, Richard Nixon made himself acceptable to the Insiders of the Establishment with an article in the October 1967 issue of *Foreign Affairs*.[14] In it, he called for a new policy of openness toward Red China, a policy which he himself later initiated in 1972.

The April 1974 issue of *Foreign Affairs* carried a very explicit recommendation for carrying out the world-government scheme of CFR founder Edward Mandell House. Authored by State Department veteran and Columbia University Professor Richard N. Gardner (himself a CFR member), "The Hard Road to World Order" admits that a single leap into world government via an organization like the United Nations is unrealistic.[15]

Instead, Gardner urged the continued piecemeal delivery of our nation's sovereignty to a variety of international organizations. He called for "an end run around national sovereignty, eroding it piece by piece." That means an end to our nation's sovereignty.

And he named as organizations to accomplish his goal the International Monetary Fund, the World Bank, the General Agreement on Tariffs and Trade, the Law of the Sea Conference, the World Food Conference, the World Population Conference, disarmament programs, and a United Nations military force. This approach,

Gardner said, "can produce some remarkable concessions of sovereignty that could not be achieved on an across-the-board basis."

Richard Gardner's preference for destroying the freedom and independence of the United States in favor of the CFR's goal of world government thoroughly dominates top circles in our nation today. The men who would scrap our nation's Constitution are praised as "progressives" and "far-sighted thinkers." The only question that remains among these powerful Insiders is which method to use to carry out their treasonous plan.

The Trilateral Angle

Unfortunately, the Council on Foreign Relations is not the only group proposing an end to the sovereignty of the United States. In 1973, another organization which now thoroughly dominates the Carter administration first saw the light of day. Also based in New York City, this one is called the Trilateral Commission.

The Trilateral Commission's roots stem from the book *Between Two Ages*[16] written by Zbigniew Brzezinski in 1970. The following quotations from that book show how closely Brzezinski's thinking parallels that of CFR founder Edward Mandell House.

On page 72, Brzezinski writes: "Marxism is simultaneously a victory of the external, active man over the inner, passive man and a victory of reason over belief."

On page 83, he states: "Marxism, disseminated on the popular level in the form of Communism, represented a major advance in man's ability to conceptualize his relationship to his world."

And on page 123, we find: "Marxism supplied

the best available insight into contemporary reality."

Nowhere does Mr. Brzezinski tell his readers that the Marxism "in the form of Communism," which he praises, has been responsible for the murder of approximately 100 million human beings in the Twentieth Century, has brought about the enslavement of over a billion more, and has caused want, privation and despair for all but the few criminals who run the communist-dominated nations.

On page 198, after discussing America's shortcomings, Brzezinski writes: "America is undergoing a new revolution" which "unmasks its obsolescence." We disagree; America is not becoming obsolete.

On page 260, he proposes "Deliberate management of the American future...with the...planner as the key social legislator and manipulator." The central planning he wants for our country is a cardinal underpinning of communism and the opposite of the way things are done in a free country.

On page 296, Mr. Brzezinski suggests piecemeal "Movement toward a larger community of the developed nations ... through a variety of indirect ties and already developing limitations on national sovereignty." Here, we have the same proposal that has been offered by Richard Gardner in the CFR publication *Foreign Affairs*.

Brzezinski then calls for the forging of community links among the United States, Western Europe, and Japan; and the extension of these links to more advanced communist countries. Finally, on page 308 of his 309-page book, he lets us know that what he really wants is "the goal of world government."

A Meeting of Minds

Zbigniew Brzezinski's *Between Two Ages* was published in 1970 while he was a professor in New York City. What happened, quite simply, is that David Rockefeller read the book. And, in 1973, Mr. Rockefeller launched the new Trilateral Commission whose purposes include linking North America, Western Europe, and Japan "in their economic relations, their political and defense relations, their relations with developing countries, and their relations with communist countries."[17]

The original literature of the Trilateral Commission also states, exactly as Brzezinski's book had proposed, that the more advanced communist states could become partners in the alliance leading to world government. In short, David Rockefeller implemented Brzezinski's proposal. The only change was the addition of Canada, so that the Trilateral Commission presently includes members from North America, Western Europe, and Japan, not just the United States, Western Europe, and Japan.

Then, David Rockefeller hired Zbigniew Brzezinski away from Columbia University and appointed him to be the director of the Trilateral Commission. Later, in 1973, the little-known former Governor of Georgia, Jimmy Carter, was invited to become a founding member of the Trilateral Commission. When asked about this relationship, Mr. Carter stated:

> Membership on this Commission has provided me with a splendid learning opportunity, and many of the members have helped me in my study of foreign affairs.[18]

We don't doubt that for a minute!

Carter's Trilateral Team

When Jimmy Carter won the nomination of the Democratic Party, he chose CFR member and Trilateralist Walter Mondale to be his running mate. Then, the man who told America that he would clean the Insiders out chose Cyrus Vance, W. Michael Blumenthal, and Harold Brown for the top three cabinet posts, and each of these men is a Trilateralist, as well as a CFR member. Other Trilateralists appointed by Mr. Carter include Zbigniew Brzezinski as National Security Advisor; Andrew Young as Ambassador to the United Nations; Richard N. Gardner as Ambassador to Italy; and several others as top government officials.

The membership list of the Trilateral Commission now notes seventeen "Former Members in Public Service" including Carter, Mondale, Vance, etc. Their places on the Commission have been taken by other influential Americans so that approximately eighty Americans, along with ten Canadians, ninety Western Europeans, and seventy-five Japanese are members today. Among the current Trilateralists can be found six senators; four congressmen; two governors; Hedley Donovan, the editor-in-chief of *Time* Incorporated; Winston Lord, president of the Council on Foreign Relations; William E. Brock, chairman of the Republican National Committee; and Dr. Henry Kissinger.[19]

As with the CFR, we do not believe that every member of the Trilateral Commission is fully committed to the destruction of the United States. Some of these men actually believe that the world would be a better place if the United States would give up its independence in the interests of world government. Others go along for the ride, a ride which means a ticket to fame, comfortable living, and constant flattery. Some, of course, really do run things and really do want to scrap our nation's independence.

On March 21, 1978, the *New York Times* featured an article about Zbigniew Brzezinski's close relationship with the President.[20] In part, it reads:

> The two men met for the first time four years ago when Mr. Brzezinski was executive director of the Trilateral Commission ... and had the foresight to ask the then obscure former Governor of Georgia to join its distinguished ranks. Their initial teacher-student relationship blossomed during the campaign and appears to have grown closer still.

The teacher in this relationship praises Marxism, thinks the United States is becoming obsolete, and is the brains behind a scheme to end the sovereignty of the United States for the purpose of building a world government. And the student is the President of the United States.

What It All Means

Let's summarize the situation we have been describing in three short statements.

1. President Carter, who was a member of the Insider-controlled Trilateral Commission as early as 1973, repeatedly told the nation during the 1976 political campaign that he was going to get rid of the Establishment Insiders if he became President. But when he took office, he promptly

filled his administration with members of the Council on Foreign Relations and the Trilateral Commission, the most prominent Insider organizations in America.

2. The Council on Foreign Relations was conceived by a Marxist, Edward Mandell House, for the purpose of creating a one-world government by destroying the freedom and independence of all nations, especially including our own. Its chairman of the board is David Rockefeller. And its members have immense control over our government and much of American life.

3. The Trilateral Commission was conceived by Zbigniew Brzezinski, who praises Marxism, who thinks the United States is becoming obsolete, and who also wants to create a one-world government. Its founder and driving force is also David Rockefeller. And it, too, exercises extraordinary control over the government of the United States.

The effect of the Council on Foreign Relations and the Trilateral Commission on the affairs of our nation is easy to see. Our own government no longer acts in its own interest; we no longer win any wars we fight; and we constantly tie ourselves to international agreements, pacts and conventions. And, our leaders have developed blatant preferences for Communist USSR, Communist Cuba, and Communist China, while they continue to work for world government, which has always been the goal of communism.

The Insider domination of our government is why America's leaders now give the backs of their hands to anti-communist nations such as South Korea, Rhodesia, Chile and our loyal allies in Taiwan. These few nations do not want to join with communists in a world government, and therefore, they are being suppressed. In short, our government has become pro-communist.

More Observations

The Carter administration, unfortunately, is only the current manifestation of this problem that has infected our nation for decades. Previous administrations, however, have carefully pretended to be anti-communist and pro-American. But there is very little pretense in an administration which arranges to give the Panama Canal to a communist-dominated government in Panama, and pays the Reds $400 million to take it. Or, when our President turns his back on America's allies in China and diplomatically recognizes the Red Chinese, who run the most brutal tyranny on earth. Or, when our President continues to disarm and weaken the United States, even as he presses for more aid and trade with Red China and Red Russia.

The foreign policy of the Carter administration, which is totally dominated by CFR and Trilateral Commission members, could hardly be worse. But the domestic policies of our government also fit into the scheme to weaken the United States and destroy the freedom of our people. Government-caused inflation continues to weaken the dollar and destroy the economy of our nation. Federal controls continue to hamstring America's productive might. And the Carter energy policy can be summed up very simply as a program to deny America the use of its own energy resources and to bring this nation to its knees through shortages and dependence on foreign suppliers.

The real goal of our own government's leaders is to make the United States into a carbon copy of a communist state, and then to merge all nations into a one-world system run by a powerful few. And in 1953, one of the individuals committed to exactly that goal said as much in a very explicit way.

That individual was H. Rowan Gaither, a CFR member who was the president of the very powerful Ford Foundation. It was during the preliminary stages of a congressional investigation into the activities of the huge tax-exempt foundations that Mr. Gaither invited Norman Dodd, the director of research for the congressional committee, to Ford Foundation headquarters in New York City. The purpose of the meeting was to discuss the reasons why Congress wanted to investigate the foundations. At the meeting, Rowan Gaither brazenly told Norman Dodd that he and others who had worked for the State Department, the United Nations, and other federal agencies had for years

> ...operated under directives issued by the White House, the substance of which was that we should make every effort to so alter life in the United States as to make possible a comfortable merger with the Soviet Union.

Then he added, "We are continuing to be guided by just such directives."

When the thoroughly shocked Norman Dodd asked Rowan Gaither if he would repeat that statement to the full House Committee so that the American people would know exactly what such powerful individuals were trying to accomplish, Gaither said: "This we would not think of doing."[21]

As further proof of just how powerful these subversive influences already were in the early

1950s, the committee, headed by Congressman Carroll Reece of Tennessee, never did get to the bottom of its investigation of the tax-exempt foundations,[22] and it was soon disbanded. A summary of what was learned appears in Rene Wormser's book, *Foundations, Their Power And Influence.*[23]

"World Order" Nightmare

But the drive toward a merger of the United States with communism continues. The final goal, as we have already stated, is a world government ruled by a powerful few. And lest anyone think that such a development will be beneficial to the world or agreeable to himself, let us list four certain consequences of world government.

One: Rather than improve the standard of living for other nations, world government will mean a forced redistribution of all wealth and a sharp reduction in the standard of living for Americans.

Two: Strict regimentation will become commonplace, and there will no longer be any freedom of movement, freedom of worship, private property rights, free speech, or the right to publish.

Three: World government will mean that this once glorious land of opportunity will become another socialistic nightmare where no amount of effort will produce a just reward.

Four: World order will be enforced by agents of the world government in the same way that agents of the Kremlin enforce their rule throughout Soviet Russia today.

That is not the kind of a world that anyone should have to tolerate. And it is surely not the kind of an existence that a parent should leave for a child. Yet, that is what is on our near horizon right now, unless enough Americans stop it.

Or a Better World

The John Birch Society was organized in part to stop the drive toward world government. In 1966, Robert Welch, the founder and leader of The John Birch Society, delivered a speech which he called *The Truth In Time*.[24]

One of the most important sections in this valuable survey is Robert Welch's discussion of the individuals who are carrying out the Conspiracy's goals, but who have never been communists. Mr. Welch coined a word to describe these powerful men. He called them the Insiders.

Strangely enough, we have seen that Jimmy Carter attacked what he, too, called Insiders during his campaign for the office of President. We are, however, making no inference that Mr. Carter used the word because Robert Welch had. The amazing aspect of this coincidence is that, in using the word "Insiders," both Jimmy Carter and Robert Welch were referring to the same individuals, and to the same force. But Jimmy Carter had obviously thrown in his lot with them, and was dishonestly seeking votes by condemning them.

Robert Welch, on the other hand, has condemned the Insiders, named the Insiders, and formed the John Birch Society to stop what they are doing to our country and to the world.

The Insiders must be stopped. The control they have over our government must be broken. And the disastrous policies of our leaders must be changed. The way to accomplish these urgent tasks is to expose the Insiders and their conspiracy. The American people must be made aware of what is happening to our country and who is doing it. If sufficient awareness can be created in time, the Insiders and their whole sinister plan will be stopped. This is the goal of The John Birch Society. Education is our strategy and truth is our weapon.[25] But more hands are needed to do the job. More hands are needed to wake the town and tell the people.

You don't have to be political scientist, or an economist, or a Ph.D. in world history to be a member of The John Birch Society. The most important single requirement has always been a sense of right and wrong, and a preference for what is right. If you want to do your part to save your country, and to stop the Insider-controlled drive toward a communist-style world government, then you ought to join the Society now.

The John Birch Society has the organization, the experience, the tools, and the determination to get the job done. God help us all if, for want of willing hands, we fail!

Notes

1. John T. Flynn, *While You Slept* (New York: Devin-Adair, 1951, and Boston: Western Islands, 1965).
2. Robert Welch, *May God Forgive Us* (Chicago: Regnery, 1952) and *Again May God Forgive Us* (Boston, Belmont Publishing Co., 1963).
3. *Human Cost Of Communism In China*, Report issued by Senate Subcommittee to Investigate the Administration of the Internal Security Act and Other Internal Security Laws, Ninety-Second Congress, 1971.
4. Nathaniel Weyl, *Red Star Over Cuba* (New York: Devin-Adair, 1960).
5. Richard L. Turner, *"I'll Never Lie To You"* — *Jimmy Carter In His Own Words* (New York:

Ballantine Books, 1976).

6. Sam Smith, "Carter's Crimson Tide," *Boston Globe*, January 29, 1978.

7. Dan Smoot, *The Invisible Government* (Boston: Western Islands, 1977).

8. *Philip Dru: Administrator* (New York: B.W. Huebsch, 1912).

9. Karl Marx, *The Communist Manifesto* (Boston: American Opinion, 1974).

10. Dan Smoot, *The Invisible Government*.

11. The 11 United States senators listed as members of the Council on Foreign Relations in 1978 are: Howard H. Baker; John C. Culver; Daniel P. Moynihan; Claiborne Pell; Jacob K. Javits; Charles McC. Mathias, Jr.; George McGovern; Abraham Ribicoff; William V. Roth, Jr.; Paul S. Sarbanes; and Adlai E. Stevenson III. See *Annual Report 1977-1978*, Council on Foreign Relations, Inc., New York.

12. June 1978 By-Laws of the Council on Foreign Relations, Article II: "It is an express condition of membership in the Council, to which condition every member accedes by virtue of his membership, that members will observe such rules and regulations as may be prescribed from time to time by the Board of Directors concerning the conduct of Council meetings or the attribution of statements made therein, and that any disclosure, publication, or other action by a member in contravention thereof may be regarded by the Board of Directors in its sole discretion as ground for termination or suspension of membership pursuant to Article I of the By-Laws." *Annual Report 1977-1978*.

13. Examples of former CFR members who did what they could to expose the purposes of the organization are former Assistant Secretary of State

Spruille Braden (see Dan Smoot, *The Invisible Government*) and retired Rear Admiral Chester Ward (see Phyllis Schlafly and Chester Ward, *Kissinger On The Couch*, New York: Arlington House, 1975).

14. Richard Nixon, "Asia After Vietnam," *Foreign Affairs*, October 1967.

15. Richard N. Gardner, "The Hard Road to World Order," *Foreign Affairs*, April 1974.

16. Zbigniew Brzezinski, *Between Two Ages* (New York: Viking Press, 1970, and New York: Penguin Books, 1976).

17. Report of Purposes and Objectives, by Trilateral Commission, March 15, 1973.

18. Jimmy Carter, *Why Not The Best?* (Nashville: Broadman Press, 1975).

19. Membership list of the Trilateral Commission, January 31, 1978.

20. Terence Smith, "Brzezinski, Foreign Policy Advisor, Sees Role as Stiffening U.S. Position," *New York Times*, March 21, 1978.

21. Norman Dodd in letter to Howard E. Kershner, December 29, 1962.

22. *Tax-Exempt Foundations*, Report of the Special House Committee to Investigate Tax-Exempt Foundations (Reece Committee), Eighty-Third Congress, 1954.

23. Rene A. Wormser, *Foundations, Their Power And Influence* (New York: Devin-Adair, 1958).

24. Robert Welch, *The Truth In Time* (Boston: American Opinion, 1966).

25. Robert Welch, *The Blue Book of The John Birch Society* (Boston: Western Islands, 1959).

Part II — 1983

The John Birch Society's survey entitled *The Insiders* was released early in 1979. Over 1,200 copies (of the filmstrip version) were purchased and put into use by members in a matter of months. Several hundred thousand copies of the printed text, in booklet form, were also purchased and distributed throughout the nation. In addition, reprint permission was granted to several other publishers, and their efforts undoubtedly doubled the readership of this analysis of the powerful few who dictate American policy.

It is impossible to know how many Americans saw or read *The Insiders* or one of the many similar treatises which paralleled it or were stimulated by it. Millions, for sure. Tens of millions, most likely.

By early 1980, the accumulated exposure of the Trilateral Commission and the Council on Foreign Relations, the two most identifiable Insider organizations, had begun to produce some dramatic effects. For one, these organizations became well enough known to be "hot topics" on the campaign circuit. Informed voters from coast to coast, especially those who were disenchanted with the Carter administration, began to seek candidates who were not tied to either of these groups.

In New Hampshire, for instance, where the first presidential primary is held every fourth February, most of the candidates for the Republican nomination were happily responding to voters that they were "not now and never have been" members of David Rockefeller's Trilateral Commission or his Council on Foreign Relations. But

Republican candidates George Bush and John Anderson could not join in such a response because each had connections to both of these elitist organizations.

This issue was not confined solely to New Hampshire either. It was a nationwide phenomenon. Witness a February 8, 1980 article in the *New York Times*.[26] Reporting on a Ronald Reagan campaign trip through the South during the first week of February, the article stated that Mr. Reagan had attacked President Carter's foreign policy because he had found that "19 key members of the Administration are or have been members of the Trilateral Commission." It also noted that when Mr. Reagan was pressed to back up his charge, an aide listed the names of President Carter, Vice President Mondale, Secretary of State Vance, Secretary of Defense Brown, and fifteen other Carter officials.

The report further stated that Reagan advisor Edwin Meese told the reporters: "...all of these people come out of an international economic-industrial organization with a pattern of thinking on world affairs." He made the very interesting comment that their influence led to a "softening" of our nation's defense capability. Both he and Mr. Reagan could have added that practically all of these Carter administration officials were also members of the Council on Foreign Relations. But neither chose to do so.

Anti-Elitist Reversals
The history of that period shows that Ronald Reagan exploited this issue very capably. On February 26th, in New Hampshire where the matter had become the deciding issue in the primary, vot-

ers gave him a lopsided victory. His strong showing and the correspondingly weak showing by George Bush delighted the nation's conservatives and set a pattern for future victories that carried Mr. Reagan all the way to the White House.

But something else happened on February 26, 1980 that should have raised many more eyebrows than it did. On the very day that Ronald Reagan convincingly won the nation's first primary, he replaced his campaign manager with longtime Council on Foreign Relations member William J. Casey. Mr. Casey served as the Reagan campaign manager for the balance of the campaign, and was later rewarded with an appointment as Director of the Central Intelligence Agency.

The selection of William J. Casey in the strategically important position of campaign manager was highly significant. He is a New York lawyer who served the Nixon administration in several positions including Under Secretary of State for Economic Affairs and Chairman of the Export-Import Bank. In those two posts especially, he gained a reputation as a crusader for U.S. taxpayer-financed aid and trade with communist nations.

During this same period, while serving as an official of the State Department, Casey declared in a public speech given in Garden City, New York that he favored U.S. policies leading to interdependence among nations and to the sacrificing of our nation's independence.[27] These attitudes are thoroughly in agreement with the long-term objectives of the Insiders, but are not at all consistent with the public positions taken by Mr. Reagan. But very few made note of the

Casey appointment because very few knew anything about Mr. Casey.

With CFR member William J. Casey on the team, the Reagan campaign was still able to focus attention on the Trilateral Commission and on fellow Republican George Bush's ties to it. But nothing was said about the older, larger, and more dangerously influential Council on Foreign Relations.

Rockefeller Ties

In April 1980, Mr. Reagan told an interviewer from the *Christian Science Monitor*[28] that he would shun the directions of David Rockefeller's Trilateral Commission. But George Bush, who had recently resigned both from the Trilateral Commission and from the board of directors of the Council on Foreign Relations, could not shake the stigma of his Insider connection.

In Florida, understanding about the Trilateral Commission led to widespread use of a political advertisement which claimed, "The same people who gave you Jimmy Carter want now to give you George Bush."[29] An identical ad appeared in Texas. The Reagan bandwagon, propelled in part by its attack on the Insiders, began to score one primary victory after another.

Eventually, Ronald Reagan convincingly won the Republican nomination. Conservatives across the nation were delighted. That is, they were delighted until he shocked his supporters by selecting George Bush as his running mate. George Bush was the very epitome of the Insider Establishment type that had made so many of these people strong Reagan backers in the first place. That night, at the Republican convention, the word "betrayal" was in common usage.

Ronald Reagan had repeatedly and publicly promised that he would pick a running mate who shared his well-known conservative views. But, of all the Republicans available, he picked the man who was the darling of the Rockefellers. Nor was the Rockefeller-Bush relationship any secret.

Campaign finance information had already revealed that prior to December 31, 1979, the Bush for President campaign had received individual $1,000 contributions (the highest amount allowed by law) from David Rockefeller, Edwin Rockefeller, Helen Rockefeller, Laurance Rockefeller, Mary Rockefeller, Godfrey Rockefeller, and several other Rockefeller relatives and employees.

Staunch Reagan supporters frantically tried to stop the Bush nomination. But political considerations quickly forced them to go along. One after another, they began to state that their man was still at the top of the ticket. "It was Reagan-Bush, not Bush-Reagan," they said. But all had to admit that the issue of Trilateral domination of the Carter administration could hardly be used with a Trilateralist veteran like Bush on the ticket.

From the time William Casey joined the Reagan team in February, the issue of CFR domination of America could not be used. And when George Bush was tapped as the Reagan running mate, the Trilateral issue was also dead. Only a very few realized that when those two issues were lost, the hope that future President Reagan would keep Insiders from key positions in government was also lost.

As the summer of 1980 faded into fall, Insiders were showing up in every conceivable part of the Reagan campaign. In September, a casual "Prelude to Victory" party was given by the Reagans at their rented East Coast home in Middleburg, Virginia. A photo taken at the party shows that the place of honor, at Mr. Reagan's immediate right, was given to none other than David Rockefeller, the leader of the CFR and the Trilateral Commission. Guests at this party included Dr. Henry Kissinger and other CFR and Trilateral members.[30]

Two weeks before the election, the front page of the *New York Times* carried a photo showing the future President campaigning in Cincinnati. Alongside him as his foreign policy advisors who the President said would answer questions for him, were Senator Howard Baker, former Ambassador Anne Armstrong, and former Secretaries of State William P. Rogers and Henry Kissinger. All were members of either the CFR or the Trilateral Commission or both.[31]

Stacking the Cabinet

Election Day 1980 produced a Reagan landslide. Caught up in misguided euphoria, conservatives began talking about the return of fiscal and diplomatic sanity to the federal government. But the shock they felt when their man had chosen George Bush as his running mate returned when President-elect Reagan announced his selections for the new cabinet.

For Secretary of State, he chose Alexander Haig, a member of the Council on Foreign Relations. For Secretary of the Treasury, Donald Regan, and for Secretary of Commerce, Malcolm Baldrige — both members of the Council on Foreign Relations. Back in February, Edwin Meese had told reporters that Mr. Reagan opposed the

Trilateral Commission because the organization's influence led to a "softening of defense." Yet, he chose for his Secretary of Defense, Caspar Weinberger, a member of the Trilateral Commission. Men from the same Insider team were still in power!

Five months after Mr. Reagan had been sworn in as President, the Council on Foreign Relations noted in its *Annual Report* that 257 of its members were serving as U.S. government officials As in previous administrations, these individuals filled many of the important Assistant Secretary and Deputy Secretary posts at the State Department, Defense Department, Treasury Department, and so on.

For the critically important post of White House Chief of Staff, Mr. Reagan named James Baker III. The White House Chief of Staff determines who gets to see the President, what reading material will appear on his desk, and what his policy options might be on any given situation. But James Baker had fought against Ronald Reagan as the campaign manager for George Bush in 1980, and as a campaign staffer for Gerald Ford in 1976. He is a confirmed liberal who was an opponent of the philosophy enunciated by Mr. Reagan during the 1980 campaign. In his White House post, he leads a team of like-minded men who have virtually isolated the President from the many conservatives who supported his election bid.

Policy Reversals

As President, Mr. Reagan has been given the image of a tough anti-communist and a frugal budget-cutter. But the images do not hold up under close scrutiny. Only one year after taking office, he acquiesced in the taxpayer-funded bailout of Poland's indebtedness to large international banks. Even worse, he skirted the law which mandates that any nation in such financial difficulty must be formally declared in default before the U.S. government could assume its debts. What made this action doubly revealing was that it occurred at the very time that thousands of Polish citizens had been incarcerated in a typical communist crackdown against even a slight semblance of freedom.

During 1981 and 1982, Ronald Reagan personally signed authorizations for the U.S. Export-Import Bank to finance nuclear steam turbines for communist Rumania and power generation equipment and a steel plant for communist China.[32] Tens of millions of U.S. taxpayers' dollars are being provided for the industrialization of these Red tyrannies.

Also, Reagan administration officials announced plans to sell arms to Red China; they told anti-communist businessmen in El Salvador that the U.S. would oppose efforts by any anti-communist Salvadorans to gain control of their country; and these same administration officials refused to honor a pledge to supply Free Chinese on Taiwan with the fighter planes deemed necessary by the Chinese for defense.

When the President authorized a joint Peking-Washington communique which stated that military support for the Free Chinese is no longer our nation's "long term policy," even CFR member Dan Rather of CBS News called the document a startling reversal of frequently stated Reagan rhetoric.

On the domestic front, the record of reversals is just as dramatic. When Mr. Reagan campaigned against Jimmy Carter, he said he would cut two percent ($13 billion) from the fiscal 1981 budget which he would inherit if elected.[33] He did nothing about that budget. Instead, he went to work immediately on the budget for the following year.

On February 18, 1981, in one of his first speeches to the nation as President, he delivered his own budget proposals. In that address, he stated: "It is important to note that we are reducing the *rate of increase* in taxing and spending. We are not attempting to cut either spending or taxing to a level below that which we presently have." (Emphasis added.) Yet, America was inundated with propaganda which had practically everyone believing that the Reagan economic package contained a substantial reduction in federal spending. Supposed budget cuts were labelled "massive," "drastic," "historic," and "cruel." But simple arithmetic showed that what President Reagan proposed for fiscal 1982 was $40 billion more spending than could be found in the 1981 budget. By the end of fiscal 1982, instead of being reduced as candidate Reagan had promised, that figure had grown to a $70 billion increase over spending from 1981. And the deficit associated with it soared to $110 billion.

But the Reagan reputation, which had been gained by his campaign oratory and by erroneous descriptions of his economic program, continued to delight conservatives and anger liberals. At a press conference one year later on March 31, 1982, a reporter asked the President to respond to the accusation that he cared little for the nation's poor. Part of his lengthy response included the following statement: "Maybe this is the time with all the talk that's going around to expose once and for all the fairy tale, the myth, that we somehow are, overall, cutting government spending.... We're not gutting the programs for the needy." He then heatedly boasted that federal spending for student loans, welfare, meals, rents, job training, and social security was higher than it had been under Jimmy Carter's last budget.

It was the Reagan-led conservative philosophy that won a decisive victory in the 1980 elections. Promises to get tough with the communists, to cut spending, to balance the budget, and to abolish the Departments of Education and Energy appealed to millions. But there has been no change in the government's direction. America continues to help communists and to harm our nation's anticommunist friends. Federal spending continues to grow, and deficits are skyrocketing. And the bureaucrats at the Departments of Education and Energy are still in place.

More Reagan Duplicity
At the halfway point of the Reagan four-year presidential term, the director of the Congressional Budget Office forecast budget deficits in the $150 billion range for the Reagan-directed fiscal years 1982, 1984 and 1985.[34] Others insisted that the deficits would be even higher. The largest deficit in the nation's history, prior to the Reagan administration, was $66 billion during the Ford years. Budget deficits, of course, translate into inflation, high interest rates, business slowdown, higher taxes, and unemployment. If federal spending were no more than federal revenue, if we had the benefit of a balanced budget

in other words, some of these problems would be far less severe.

Shortly after he took office, Mr. Reagan twisted the arms of conservative senators and congressmen to get them to raise the ceiling on the national debt. Had he insisted on no further increases, the spiralling growth of government could have been checked. But instead, he used his influence to authorize more debt. Then he did the very same thing again eight months later, and again in 1982. As a result, interest on the debt alone grew to $117 billion for fiscal 1982.

In his State of the Union address on January 26, 1982, President Reagan again appealed to conservative Americans when he stated:

> Raising taxes won't balance the budget. It will encourage more government spending and less private investment. Raising taxes will slow economic growth, reduce production and destroy future jobs.... So, I will not ask you to try to balance the budget on the backs of the American taxpayers. I will seek no tax increases this year.

But, in August 1982, his actions again failed to parallel his rhetoric, and he used all the muscle he could muster to get Congress to pass the largest tax increase in our nation's history — $227 billion over five years. Opponents of this huge tax increase were the principled conservatives who had supported his election bid. The President's allies on the tax increases included big-spending liberals like Senator Edward Kennedy and Speaker of the House "Tip" O'Neill.

One result of the failure of the Reagan administration to stand by the philosophy which brought the President to the White House is that conservatives everywhere have been blamed for the nation's woes. The congressional elections of 1982 amounted to a significant setback for the entire conservative movement. It seemed to many voters that the conservative program had been tried and found wanting. The truth is that the conservative program has yet to be tried. And the reason why it has not been tried is that the Insiders who surround Ronald Reagan are still in control.

The President himself supplied dramatic evidence of the existence of this control in comments he made about the $5.5 billion increase in gasoline taxes he signed into law on January 5, 1983.

At his press conference on September 28, 1982, he was asked: "Knowing of your great distaste for taxes and tax increases, can you assure the American people now that you will flatly rule out any tax increases, revenue enhancers or specifically an increase in the gasoline tax?"

Mr. Reagan responded: "Unless there's a palace coup and I'm overtaken or overthrown, no, I don't see the necessity for that. I see the necessity for more economies, more reductions in government spending...."

Less than three months later, he was vigorously promoting that increase in the gasoline tax. Call it a "palace coup" or whatever, the chain of events certainly suggests that someone other than the President is in control.

CFR Lineage

When CFR member Alexander Haig resigned as Secretary of State, CFR board member George P. Shultz was immediately named to replace him.

During confirmation hearings, several senators and a number of political writers worried openly about what became known as "the Bechtel Connection." It seemed almost sinister to them to have Mr. Shultz join another former Bechtel Corporation executive, Defense Secretary Caspar Weinberger, in the Reagan Cabinet's inner circle. But the senators and the supposedly hard-nosed, prying reporters were assured that there was no cause for alarm, and the matter died.

If a common corporate lineage of these two cabinet officials stirs concern, however, why is there no concern whatsoever over the fact that both are current members of the Council on Foreign Relations? And why not even a bare mention of the fact that Mr. Shultz would be the tenth Secretary of State in a row to hold CFR membership before or immediately after his tenure?

That the CFR owns the State Department can hardly be denied. But it can be ignored, which is precisely what has been going on in America for decades. The result? Most Americans remain totally unaware that the same powerful Insiders still control our government.

The Council on Foreign Relations rarely receives any press coverage. When confronted by adversaries, spokesmen for the organization repeatedly insist that it is merely a glorified study group which takes no positions and has no stated policy on foreign or domestic affairs. Rather, they insist, the CFR merely offers the diverse thinking given by important students of world affairs.

Yet, in an unusually frank article about the Council appearing in the *New York Times* for October 30, 1982, author Richard Bernstein obviously reflected the attitude of the CFR executives with whom he had spoken when he wrote: "It [the Council] numbers among its achievements much of the country's post World War II planning, the basic ideas for reconciliation with China and the framework for an end to military involvement in Indochina."[35]

If an organization takes no positions and has no stated policies, how can it list as "achievements" the shaping of some of our government's most important decisions over the past forty years? And what "achievements" these have been!

Post World War II planning has seen the United States descend from undisputed world leadership and the admiration of virtually all nations to being militarily threatened by the USSR and being despised by almost everyone else. Post World War II planning, for which the CFR claims credit, has seen the United States bumble its way from a defeat here to a setback there to an error in judgment somewhere else, while freedom has retreated everywhere and the world increasingly falls under communist control.

Reconciliation with China, rather than being an achievement, puts our nation in bed with the world's most brutal tyranny and is making us adversaries of the friendly, productive, free and honorable Chinese on Taiwan.

Nor is the disgraceful conclusion to our military involvement in Indochina anything of which to be proud. The end saw three nations — Laos, Cambodia and South Vietnam — fall to typically brutal communist tyranny. The toll in human slaughter which has followed in the wake of our nation's pullout from Southeast Asia is indescribable. And those who said that these nations would not fall like dominoes are now strangely silent.

It is highly significant to see this corroboration of our long-held belief that the CFR helps to shape our nation's policies. The policies noted in Bernstein's *New York Times* article have produced communist victories in every case. It is, therefore, even more significant to have this admission of the remarkable dovetailing of CFR and communist goals.

Double Jeopardy Elitism

The Trilateral Commission also attempts to convey the impression that it exists simply as a high-level discussion group which merely fosters economic and political cooperation. In 1982, the Commission released *East-West Trade At A Crossroads*, which it quickly claimed contained only the views of its authors.[36]

This study recommends an increase in the trade with communist nations that fuels their military capabilities. Even after noting that the communist bloc nations are already heavily in debt to the West, and that previous trade had "produced no significant change in the foreign policy of the Soviet Union," the study also recommends supplying even more credit to stimulate greater trade. That credit, of course, is to be supplied by America's taxpayers. Nor is this any departure from previously held positions published by the Commission, or enunciated by its members.

What is most significant is that the recommendations given by this Trilateral Commission report are wholly in tune with the policies both of the U.S. government and the governments of the communist bloc nations. The American people *do* supply the communist nations with equipment, technology and credit, even while communist troops crush Poland and ravage Afghanistan, and while Soviet missiles are menacing the United States. What this Trilateral Commission publication recommends is no less consistent with Soviet desires than have been the so-called achievements of the Council on Foreign Relations.

The Insiders of the Council on Foreign Relations and the newer Trilateral Commission have been controlling U.S. policy for decades. Unfortunately, these same individuals are still running things, despite the fact that the nomination and election of Ronald Reagan can be substantially attributed to a growing national revulsion at years of Insider control of this nation.

The Reagan Enigma

How then can one explain Ronald Reagan, the man on whom so many Americans placed such great hope? All we can say is that there are several theories to choose from, all of which fall in the realm of speculation.

One theory holds that he is a good man with fine instincts and excellent intentions, but is such a hater of confrontation that he has effectively been steamrolled by the non-conservatives who surround him.

Another theory holds that he was never a real conservative in the first place, but is a very capable orator who can read a good speech and produce a convincing image. The United Republicans of California published such a view in 1975, after having experienced all of the years that Ronald Reagan governed their state.[37]

One individual who shares the view that Mr. Reagan's political effect has never been conservative is Thomas Gale Moore of Stanford University's Hoover Institution. In a syndicated column appearing in May 1981,[38] he discussed the much-publicized Reagan plans to cut spending and reduce bureaucratic regulation. But Mr. Moore then cautioned:

> Skeptics find President Reagan's record as governor, often alluded to during the campaign, far from reassuring, especially since he used much the same rhetoric during his gubernatorial campaigns as appeared later during his campaign for the presidency.
>
> While in Sacramento, he converted the state income tax into one of the most progressive in the nation, introduced withholding taxes, raised sales taxes, and sharply increased taxes on business.
>
> While he was in office, California government expenditures increased faster than was typical of other states. Notwithstanding his campaign rhetoric, welfare expenditures alone escalated 61 percent in real terms during his two terms as governor.

That is hardly a record that should merit the label "conservative."

A third theory would excuse the President by holding that government is out of control in the fiscal sense, and that previously arranged international entanglements are so binding that not even a President can reverse runaway spending or call a halt to the increasingly obvious pro-communist stance taken by Washington. Happily, there are not too many who believe that this theory has any validity.

Finally, another theory, which is not inconsistent with certain aspects of the first two given above, is that, while Ronald Reagan is indeed the President, he is not the boss. Nor have a number of his predecessors really been in charge. Instead, the Insiders who really run America select a man whom they then permit to occupy the White House. But it is they who still run the government through like-minded individuals with whom they surround the President.

When Ronald Reagan announced that CFR member Donald Regan was to be his Secretary of the Treasury, an aide pointed out that Mr. Regan had donated $1,000, the maximum personal contribution allowed by law, to Jimmy Carter's re-election campaign. And that, in 1980, Donald Regan had also contributed to and raised money for left-wing congressmen who were engaged in tight races with conservative, Reagan-backed challengers. When an aide asked then President-elect Reagan why he would choose a man with such a background, Mr. Reagan is reported to have said: "Why didn't anyone tell me?"[39]

Why indeed did Ronald Reagan place Donald Regan in his cabinet? We suggest that he did not make the selection, but that the Insiders made it and have made many others, and that such a practice has been the rule rather than the exception for years.

In late 1960, when John Kennedy formed his cabinet, his selections included Robert McNamara for Secretary of Defense. At a gathering prior to their taking office, Mr. Kennedy had to be introduced to Mr. McNamara. Could he logically have picked a man to be Secretary of Defense whom he had never met? Or, is it not more reasonable to assume that the selection had been made for him? As Secretary of Defense, Robert McNamara did a great deal to destroy our nation's then-unchallenged military advantage.

Time magazine reported that Richard Nixon selected Henry Kissinger for the White House post of Director of National Security based on having once met him at a cocktail party, and having read one of his books. Yet, CFR member Henry Kissinger was widely reported to have wept publicly when his patron Nelson Rockefeller lost the 1968 Republican nomination to Richard Nixon. Did Nixon choose Kissinger? Or, were the reports in *U.S. News & World Report* and elsewhere correct when they openly stated the Rockefellers placed Kissinger in the Nixon administration's inner circle?

Routing the Insiders

There is, of course, nothing wrong with any President relying on the advice of others in selecting his top assistants. What is vitally important is whose advice is being followed, what type of individuals are named to the positions, and what they do with the power given to them.

It is our view, as we implied earlier, that a tightly knit and very powerful group has run America far more than has any recent President. Its effect on our nation has been horrible. We call this group *The Insiders* and we dare to label their activity a conspiracy — a conspiracy that must be exposed and routed if the disastrous national policies of the past several decades are to be reversed.

The route that must be followed in order to accomplish this reversal must begin by placing the mass of evidence about this conspiracy before the American people. A well-informed public will then work to see that it is represented by men and women at the congressional level who will not be intimidated or corrupted by Insider influence in government, the press, the academic world, the big labor unions, or anywhere else. The Insiders may indeed have working control of the Presidency and the mechanisms for choosing a President, but their clout at the congressional and senatorial levels is a great deal less and exists largely through bluff. In time, a sufficiently aware public can even break the Insiders' grip on the White House itself.

Will America continue on a path which amounts to fiscal suicide? Will our government continue to build and support communism everywhere, while it works simultaneously to destroy the few remaining anti-communist nations? The John Birch Society wants to put an end to Insider control of the policies of this nation. If we are to succeed, the active help of many more Americans is needed in a massive educational crusade. Whether or not you decide to help will count heavily toward whether the future for this nation will be enslavement or freedom.

The Insiders are hoping that you will do nothing. But true Americans everywhere are asking for and counting on your help. The best kind of help you can give is active support for and membership in The John Birch Society.

Notes

26. "Reagan Steps Up Attack on Carter's Foreign Policy," *New York Times*, February 8, 1980.

27. "The Reshaping of the World Economy," an address by Acting Secretary of State William J. Casey at Adelphi University, March 3, 1974.

28. Kevin Phillips, "The Strange Tale of How Ronald Reagan Sold Out to the Trilateralist-tinged Republican Establishment," *Los Angeles Herald-Examiner*, August 4, 1980.

29. *Newsweek*, March 24, 1980.

30. *W Magazine*, September 26, 1980.

31. James Reston, "A Day With Reagan," *New York Times*, October 27, 1980; also, *New York Times*, October 21, 1980.

32. *Federal Register*, May 29, 1981, Page 28833; *Federal Register*, September 9, 1982, Page 39655.

33. Televised address of October 24, 1980.

34. *The Review Of The News*, August 11, 1982.

35. Richard Bernstein, "An Elite Group On U.S. Policy Is Diversifying," *New York Times*, October 30, 1982.

36. Robert V. Roosa, Armin Gutowski, and Michaya Matsukawa, *East-West Trade At A Crossroads* (New York: Trilateral Commission, 1982).

37. *Oppose Candidacy of Reagan*, United Republicans of California, San Gabriel, California, May 4, 1975. The UROC Resolution said of Ronald Reagan that his "deeds have served the liberals"; he "doubled the State Budget and raised taxes"; he "promoted regional government contrary to his expressed philosophy of local government"; and he "betrayed conservative principles in the areas of property rights, income tax withholding, gun control, medicine, mental health, welfare reform, crime control, etc."

38. Thomas Gale Moore, "Did Liberal Hearts Beat Under GOP Conservative Clothing?", *Boston Herald-American*, May 12, 1981. Mr. Moore also showed that, after World War II, government always grew at a faster pace while Republicans occupied the White House (Eisenhower, Nixon and Ford) than it grew while Democrats held the Presidency (Truman, Kennedy and Johnson). He wrote, "In fact, the evidence suggests that a voter who wants a liberal policy should vote Repubican; if he yearns for a conservative policy, he should cast his ballot for a Democrat."

39. Gary Allen, "Regan At Treasury," *American Opinion*, February 1981.

Part III — 1992

The grip on the reins of the U.S. government possessed by the Insiders grew dramatically when George Bush entered the White House. Far from being an opponent of the powerful few who dictate America's policies, Mr. Bush is a long-standing member of the Insider clique, sometimes known simply as "the Establishment."

Staff reporter Sidney Blumenthal could write in the February 10, 1988 issue of the Insider-led *Washington Post*: "George Bush, in fact, has been a dues-paying member of the Establishment, if it is succinctly defined as the Council on Foreign Relations and the Trilateral Commission." In his article, Blumenthal noted that Mr. Bush severed his formal ties with both organizations in 1979. But the *Post* reporter sought comments about Mr. Bush's twin resignations from David Rockefeller, the powerful Insider who had been chairman of both organizations when the future President began his quest for the White House. Mr. Rockefeller told Blumenthal in 1988:

Bush has the knowledge and has the background and has had the posts. If he were President, he would be in a better position than anyone else to pull together the people in the country who believe that we are in fact living in one world and have to act that way.... I don't know what I would have done [about certain criticism for holding memberships in both the CFR and the TC]. I don't think he really accomplished what he hoped. It was still used against him. He has since spoken to the Council and the Trilateral and has been fully supportive of their activities. Even though he has resigned, he hasn't walked away from them.

Clearly, George Bush may have resigned formal memberships in the CFR and TC in 1979, but his heart was still with both organizations. On March 29, 1981, only nine weeks after he took the oath of office as Vice President, he addressed a Trilateral Commission meeting held in Washington. The next day was to have been the occasion of a meeting of Trilateral officials with President Reagan in the Oval Office. But it had to be canceled because of John Hinckley's attempt on the President's life that very morning.[40]

Early in the 1980 campaign, Mr. Bush distributed a statement about his affiliation with the Trilateral Commission. Given on "George Bush For President" stationery, it said: "I personally severed my association with the Trilateral Commission as well as with many other groups I had been involved with because I didn't have time to attend the endless conferences." Once an elected Vice President, however, he managed to find enough time even to deliver a speech at one of those "endless" Trilateral conferences.

The Bush Path to the White House

There wasn't much doubt that George Bush would receive the Republican nomination for President in 1988. For eight years, he had dutifully followed the lead set by President Ronald Reagan and all of the CFR-member appointees dominating that administration. How many CFR members were part of the Reagan-Bush team?

CFR *Annual Reports* for 1981 and 1988 show that in the early months of the Reagan Presidency, 257 CFR members held posts as U.S. government officials. By mid-1988, however, the number had risen to 313. Ronald Reagan was ultimately responsible for this growing CFR dominance, but George Bush was surely not complaining about it.

As Vice Presidents are expected to do, Mr. Bush stayed out of the limelight. He spent those years representing the United States at scores of foreign funerals, making appearances at Republican fundraising events, sitting behind Mr. Reagan in full view of the television cameras during each of the State of the Union addresses, and nodding in approval at whatever the President was saying or doing. It wasn't difficult for him because, even though Mr. Reagan had at times uttered some conservative-sounding sentiments and seemed like an opponent of the Insider Establishment, the President's actions were very much in keeping with the agenda of the Insiders. The Reagan performance rarely matched the Reagan rhetoric, and it continuously indicated that the President didn't really mean what he was saying.

Good Republican soldier George Bush was even willing to suppress his stinging characterization of candidate Reagan's 1980 economic plans as "voodoo economics." The Reagan program called for increased defense spending and decreased taxation, all of which the former California governor claimed could be accomplished while still producing a balanced budget.

Spend more, take in less, and balance the budget? While George Bush was still contesting for the 1980 Republican nomination, he was on the attack, and his choice of the word "voodoo" to describe the Reagan plan was both reasonable and colorful. When the economic reality dawned (the $110 billion deficit for fiscal 1982, the first full year of the Reagan administration, was the highest in U.S. history), one wag suggested that Reaganomics was giving voodoo a bad name.

But, as a stalwart Insider even more than as a member of the Reagan team, George Bush dutifully bit his tongue and supported the piling up of huge deficits for the next generation to shoulder — even as they grew larger and more threatening. How bad did it get? The average annual deficit for the eight years of the Reagan administration exceeded $175 billion. If the vaunted "Reagan revolution" had promised anything, it had promised fiscal responsibility. Yet, the Insiders whom Mr. Reagan placed in charge gave the nation exactly the opposite.

The fiscal profligacy was there for anyone to see. When the Republicans took office in January 1981, the accumulated national debt amassed over the 200-year history of the United States stood at $935 billion. Then, on September 30, 1988 (four months before the end of the Reagan Presidency and the end of the last full fiscal year of the Reagan era), that debt had just about tripled and stood at $2,572 billion.

During those eight years, the United States went from being the world's largest creditor nation to becoming its largest debtor. No more could we scoff at Mexico, Argentina or Brazil. We were in worse shape. The future of the American people and their nation was being mortgaged by the Insiders running the Reagan-Bush team, but George Bush's political future dictated that he keep quiet about it. And the Insider-dominated media, which should have repeatedly reminded him of his "voodoo" remark, ignored the plunge into debt and gave the impression that there wasn't anything anyone could or should do about it.

Why this conspiracy of silence? Because deficits leading to socialist control of the American people were exactly what the Insiders wanted. Because no one knew this better than the Vice President, whose ties to the Insiders were both numerous and unbroken. And because the media itself was Insider dominated.

The Loaded Resumé

There has never been a presidential candidate who could produce a more impressive — and a more Insider-connected — resumé than the one George Bush offered in 1988. He had served virtually everywhere. Other than his two terms as a Republican congressman from Houston, however, he'd been appointed by Insiders to every position he has held. With connections orchestrated early in his career by his father, Prescott Bush, a Wall Street international banking Insider who served as a liberal Republican senator from Connecticut during the 1950s, George had access to many of the "right" people.

And he had other early connections too, such as his membership in the very prestigious yet downright spooky Skull & Bones Society at Yale. According to a 1977 article in *Esquire* magazine, this little-known Society forces its members to participate in arcane rituals, maintain deep secrecy, and swear unswerving loyalty to the organization itself.[41] Each year at Yale, 15 seniors are welcomed into the group. The Skull & Bones roster lists some extremely prominent and influential Americans, many of whom are distinguished for having been lifelong internationalists. These include W. Averell Harriman, Henry Stimson, Henry Luce, McGeorge Bundy, William Bundy, Winston Lord, and Robert Lovett.

Questions to members about what goes on within Skull & Bones always go unanswered, inviting the charge that something is indeed being hidden. The late Gary Allen believed the group to be a "recruiting ground for the international banking clique, the CIA, and politics." It is hardly surprising that Mr. Bush chose Supreme Court Justice Potter Stewart to administer his oath of office as Vice President in January 1981. A 1937 graduate of Yale, Justice Stewart was himself a Skull & Bones member. A presidential candidate's membership in a secret society such as Skull & Bones ought to evoke numerous questions from the mass media and the public. But because the group is so little known, there is virtually no controversy about it or about the President's affiliation with it.

In 1970, George Bush was soundly defeated in his bid for a U.S. Senate seat from Texas. Council on Foreign Relations veteran Richard Nixon rescued him from potential obscurity by naming him U.S. Ambassador to the United Nations. The new appointee began his duties by recommending the seating of Red China alongside Nationalist China. When the UN voted to seat only the Communist Chinese, and their delegate used his maiden speech to condemn the United States, Mr. Bush expressed mere "disappointment."

A better man would have walked out of that nest of anti-American tyrants, which is exactly the response Mr. Bush once advocated. In 1964, he declared: "If Red China should be admitted to the UN, then the UN is hopeless and we should withdraw."[42] Rhetoric is one thing and, as this statement and what followed surely proves, performance is frequently quite the opposite. What is also true is that a better person than the man sitting in that UN post would never have accepted appointment to it in the first place.

How seriously our nation was hated at the UN could be gauged by the spectacle of delegates actually dancing in the aisles when the General Assembly ousted Free China, gave China's seat to the communist regime, and delivered an intentional insult to the United States. Ambassador Bush responded meekly and then proceeded to welcome the emissary of the Peking tyranny to the Security Council seat from which the anticommunist Chinese had just been expelled.

He then found no difficulty supporting Mr. Nixon's growing friendship with Peking's murderous tyrants, and he helped to make the grovelling 1972 Nixon pilgrimage to the land of Mao Tsetung and Chou En Lai a much-needed source of legitimacy for the Red Chinese regime. During that highly publicized visit, President Nixon's formal banquet toast to Chairman Mao and Premier Chou included his revealing assurance that their history-making meeting was taking place because of "the hope that each of us has to build a *new world order*." (Emphasis added.)[43] The use of the phrase was unsettling to Americans who knew that Insiders had been employing it for generations. But it didn't upset George Bush. And claims in 1991 by the White House that Mr. Bush and National Security Advisor Scowcroft had dreamed it up themselves during a boat ride off Kennebunkport in August 1990 were bald-faced lies.[44]

After Red China had been completely accepted at the United Nations, and after the future President had spent a considerable amount of his time trying to repair the UN's sagging reputation with the American people, George Bush abandoned the UN post in early 1973 to accept "election" as national chairman of the Republican Party. (This was essentially another appointment even though party regulars went through the formality of electing him.) Almost immediately, he found himself embroiled in the Watergate travails of his good friend Richard Nixon. He managed to survive that curious episode in American history although Nixon did not.

Then, given his choice of posts by President Gerald Ford, whose administration was in the hands of such highly placed Insiders as Henry Kissinger, Mr. Bush opted in October 1974 to lead the U.S. Liaison Office in Peking. The Senate Internal Security Subcommittee's 1971 report entitled *Human Cost of Communism in China*[45] had detailed the systematic liquidation of tens of millions of Chinese by the forces controlled by Mao and Chou. Mass murder and other forms of inhuman treatment of the Chinese and Tibetan peoples were still going on. But none of that deterred Mr. Bush from doing what he could to provide the murderers with much-needed legitimacy. It was Insider policy to bring Mainland China into the community of nations.

President Ford then enabled Mr. Bush to add another item to his resumé by appointing him Director of the Central Intelligence Agency in December 1975. He lasted only a year at CIA because his newest patron, Gerald Ford, lost to Jimmy Carter in the 1976 Presidential race.

The final entry in the Bush resumé, of course, focussed on his eight years as Vice President under Ronald Reagan. All in all, a stunningly impressive listing of credentials: two terms in Congress; Ambassador to the UN; chairman of the Republican Party; chief of the U.S. Liaison office in Peking; CIA Director; and Vice President of the United States. These were his open credentials, the ones George Bush wanted everyone to be aware of.

Insider Credentials

But George Bush had other credentials that he kept quiet — although he wanted them known within Insider circles. He had accepted membership in the Council on Foreign Relations during 1971[46] and a place on the roster of the Trilateral Commission during 1977.[47] As all members of these elite groups always do, he avoided publicity about his Insider connections because a growing number of Americans had learned about CFR and TC goals and didn't want what each advocated.

Unlike the CFR that delights in listing its important members, the Trilateral Commission has a policy of denying or suspending membership to holders of national government posts. The group periodically publishes a list naming "Former Members in Public Service" along with its fewer than 300 members (a third each from North America, Europe and Japan). As soon as their government service is completed, however, these individuals are frequently welcomed back into the organization. Had he not been serving in government posts, Mr. Bush would likely have been tapped for Trilateral membership earlier than 1977. The Commission, formed in 1973 by CFR leaders David Rockefeller and Zbigniew Brzezinski to promote world government, was made to order for an ambitious implementer of Insider objectives.

Out of government service early in 1977, Mr. Bush immediately signed on with the Trilateral elite, and also accepted a post on the 25-member board of directors of the CFR.[48] Over the years, many CFR members have sought to defend their own participation in this world-government-promoting group by insisting that they were trying to bring a more patriotic perspective into the group's proceedings. It is safe to say, however, that no one trying to challenge the overall thrust of the CFR ended up on its board of directors.

With duties surrounding his board of directors service in the CFR and his new membership in the TC (the twin pillars of the Establishment, both led by David Rockefeller), Mr. Bush was kept very busy. But he also began spending time in Houston where he teamed up with James A. Baker III, the man who made a name for himself during the 1976 Republican sweepstakes both with his strong support for Establishment favorite Gerald Ford and his equally strong distaste for Ronald Reagan's conservative pronouncements. The two began planning for a 1980 Bush run at the White House.

Atlantic Council

Another credential Mr. Bush didn't publicize was his mid-1970s membership on the Board of Directors of the Atlantic Council of the United States (AC). Formed in the 1960s by former Secretary of State Christian Herter, the AC's formal Policy Statement, approved on May 10, 1976, was endorsed by George Bush when he became an AC board member in 1978. It claims that the changing world "can no longer be accommodated by political forms and sovereignties developed in the eighteenth and nineteenth centuries."[49]

What this means, of course, is that in the view of the Atlantic Council's planners the independent United States of America formed in the 18th century is an anachronism. The AC Policy Statement boldly enunciated a desire to form institutions "to deal adequately with problems with which no existing nation-state can cope successfully alone." In other words, let's do away with nation-states, like the United States.

Other members of the Atlantic Council's board who served alongside George Bush included such prominent Insider CFR stalwarts as Henry Kissinger, Paul Nitze, William J. Casey, Brent Scowcroft, Harlan Cleveland, and Eugene Rostow. The organization's publication *Issues and Opinions* also noted that its board of directors included "George S. Franklin Jr., Coordinator, The Trilateral Commission" and "Winston Lord, President, Council on Foreign Relations." Interlocking memberships and directorates in these Insider organizations have always been common. Insider enthusiasm for one of their own to occupy the President's office has been just as common.

An Insider in the White House

As President, Mr. Bush dutifully awarded the following key posts to Insiders of the CFR: Secretary of Defense went to Dick Cheney (like Mr. Bush, Cheney had been a CFR board member),

Secretary of the Treasury was given to Nicholas Brady, National Security Advisor to Brent Scowcroft (another CFR Board member), Attorney General to Richard Thornburgh, CIA Director to William Webster, Deputy Secretary of State to Lawrence Eagleburger, Office of Management and Budget Director to Richard Darman, Federal Reserve Chairman to Alan Greenspan, and Joint Chiefs of Staff Chairman to General Colin Powell. As of February 4, 1991, the Trilateral Commission — hardly a disqualifying credential for service on the Bush team — could proudly list as "Former Members in Public Service": George Bush, Richard Darman, Lawrence Eagleburger, Alan Greenspan, and Brent Scowcroft.

The absence of Secretary of State James A. Baker III's name from any CFR roster breaks the string of ten Secretaries of State in a row (starting with Dean Acheson in the Truman administration) who held membership in the organization. Why Baker has never been appointed, or why he has declined an invitation if one were ever offered, is unknown. He is ideologically in tune with everything the CFR wants for America and has himself chosen CFR members as his top advisors.

The Baker-led State Department shocked even its most intense critics in late April 1990 with its invitation to Tim Wheeler to be the featured speaker at a May Day luncheon in the department's plush reception rooms. At the time, Wheeler was the veteran Washington correspondent for the *People's Daily World*, the official newspaper of the Communist Party USA.[50]

With CFR members dominating State, this invitation is not too surprising. It calls to mind a revealing comment about Anatoly Dobrynin, Soviet Russia's valued ambassador to the U.S. from 1962 until 1986. A very suave spokesman for his tyrannical government, this *ex officio* head of the KGB in the United States had actually befriended many American leaders during his long stay in Washington. Writing about him in the May 13, 1984 *New York Times Magazine*, Madeline G. Kalb noted his distaste for speeches and interviews but revealed that he had always kept "in touch with influential journalists and top people at such organizations as the Council on Foreign Relations." Communist officials always found CFR leaders far more compatible than any anticommunist Americans.

According to the CFR's 1991 *Annual Report*, a whopping 382 of its members were serving as U.S. government officials. The organization's total membership numbers only 2,790, meaning that 14 percent of those who have joined this leading Insider group hold high government positions. No other remotely similar organization can claim such clout within the government. This startling dominance over the nation's affairs ought to be a burning issue, but similar CFR dominance of the mass media keeps most Americans totally unaware of who is really running the U.S. government. The Insiders, of course, hope that they remain unaware.

The "New World Order"

In keeping with his Insider credentials, President Bush grabbed at an opportunity to advance the Insider agenda. He reacted to the August 2, 1990 Iraqi attack on Kuwait by immediately sending U.S. military forces to the Middle East. He furiously gathered support for a coalition-backed effort to confront Saddam Hussein. He went to the United Nations where he supported economic sanctions against Iraq, even as he was stepping up his own anti-Hussein rhetoric and sending increasing numbers of U.S. troops into the region. He turned to the United Nations, not the U.S. Constitution to which he'd sworn a solemn oath, for authorization for his military moves. He then began to state his goals — over and over again.

- **September 11, 1990 televised address:** "Out of these troubled times, our fifth objective — a new world order — can emerge.... We are now in sight of a United Nations that performs as envisioned by its founders."
- **January 7, 1991 interview in *U.S. News & World Report*:** "I think that what's at stake here is the new world order. What's at stake here is whether we can have disputes peacefully resolved in the future by a reinvigorated United Nations."
- **January 9, 1991 Press Conference:** "[The Gulf crisis] has to do with a new world order. And that new world order is only going to be enhanced if this newly activated peacekeeping function of the United Nations proves to be effective."
- **January 16, 1991 televised address:** "When we are successful, and we will be, we have a real chance at this new world order, an order in which a credible United Nations can use its peacekeeping role to fulfill the promise and vision of the UN's founders."
- **August 1991 *National Security Strategy of the United States* issued by the**

White House and personally signed by George Bush: "In the Gulf, we saw the United Nations playing the role dreamed of by its founders.... I hope history will record that the Gulf crisis was the crucible of the new world order."

Two common themes are present in each of these pronouncements: 1. The President is clearly committed to a "new world order"; and 2. his view of this "new world order" includes boosting the prestige and power of the United Nations.

What he didn't explain is that the phrase "new world order" has been used for generations by individuals seeking to control the world. Those employing it have sought socialism (economic control) and world government (political control) over mankind.

The War for a "Reinvigorated" UN

Mr. Bush's revealing statements called for a United Nations as envisioned by its "founders." It becomes critically important, therefore, to know who these founders were. A leading member of the U.S. delegation at the founding UN conference in 1945 was Alger Hiss, later shown to have been a secret communist. There were 15 other U.S. government officials working for the establishment of the UN who were also later discovered to have been secret communists.[51] One of the more important of these was Assistant Secretary of the Treasury Harry Dexter White, the architect of the International Monetary Fund to which Mr. Bush advocates giving huge amounts of U.S. taxpayers' money.

Added to the listing of communists busily working to create the UN were 43 current or future CFR members. Men of prominence in this group included CFR founder House's protégé John Foster Dulles.[52] Also, Nelson A. Rockefeller, Adlai E. Stevenson, Edward R. Stettinius, Ralph Bunche, Philip C. Jessup, and future CFR chairman John J. McCloy.[53]

There was, of course, a delegation from the USSR. It was led by Andrei Gromyko who, along with all of his Soviet colleagues, was a communist. Other delegations from the total of 50 nations participating in the founding were top-heavy with socialists, communists, internationalists, one-worlders, and despisers of national sovereignty. There were also a few starry-eyed dreamers who believed they were participating in the founding of a totally benign peace-making organization, not something designed by its many founders as an organization meant to take control of the world.

The real "vision" of the UN founders should hardly be a mystery to anyone. All communists who have ever walked the earth have sought world government, an end to national sovereignty, the end of personal freedom, and the domination of the many by the few. And every socialist has always sought government control of everyone economically, a tactic that leads more subtly to the same goals sought by communists. The UN was literally made to order for totalitarians — which is exactly why those who seek political or economic domination worked so hard to bring the organization into being.

Also, wouldn't it be quite ridiculous to suggest that the likes of Alger Hiss, Harry Dexter White, Andrei Gromyko, John Foster Dulles, and John J.

McCloy were duped into supporting an organization that would thwart their one-world designs? These men are prime examples of those who envisioned a world run by the UN that they would control.

These UN founders, including the top Insiders of their day, wanted the U.S. in the world body and they knew that the Declaration of Independence and the U.S. Constitution would have to be scrapped along the way. Therefore, Mr. Bush's determination to use the Gulf War to see the United Nations "reinvigorated" according to the wishes of its "founders" is both revealing and frightening. His hope that the war would be the "crucible of the new world order" says it all.

Liberal Senator Paul Simon (D-IL) addressed his Senate colleagues on January 10, 1991, a few days before President Bush gave the go-ahead to unleash the U.S. military. With war a virtual certainty, he criticized the President for "giving up on the sanctions option." He said his concern was shared by others, including Senator George Mitchell (D-ME), who had earlier that same day given his opinion that the decision for war was being made prematurely. The two senators had toured the Middle East and even visited U.S. bases only three weeks earlier.

Hoping to influence the President to stick with sanctions and avoid bloodshed, Simon and Mitchell had gone immediately to the White House upon returning from their December trip and were dismayed to find Mr. Bush eager for war. Simon reported that during their conversation, the President spelled out his reason for the course he intended to pursue as follows: "If we use the military, we can make the United Nations a really meaningful effective voice for peace and stability in the future."[54]

According to the President himself, therefore, his overriding objective in sending 500,000 U.S. troops into combat was to build the clout of the United Nations. How many of the men and women wearing the uniform of this nation understood that as they were sent into battle? How many understand it today?

Even before he formally opposed Mr. Bush for the Republican nomination for President, journalist Patrick Buchanan said what many Americans had been longing to hear from a presidential candidate. Attacking the President's policies only weeks after the campaign against Saddam Hussein had begun, he wrote:

> The Trilateralist-CFR, Wall Street-Big Business elite: the neo-conservative intellectuals who dominate the think tanks and op-ed pages; the Old Left, with its one-world, collective-security, UN *uber alles* dream: All have come together behind the "new world order." Everyone is on board, or so it seems. But out there, trying to break through is the old, authentic voice of American patriotism, of nationalism, of America First, saying hell, no, we won't go.[55]

He was clearly challenging both the Insiders' goals and their favored President who was busily promoting their cause. And he refused to back down in the face of angry and vicious attacks. On December 10, 1991, in his New Hampshire speech announcing his candidacy for the nomination, Buchanan said of the President:

He is a globalist and we are nationalists. He believes in some "Pax Universalis"; we believe in the Old Republic. He would put America's wealth and power at the service of some vague new world order; we will put America first.

Dragging America Down

One of the more sinister tactics employed by socialists to gain economic control of the people involves accumulating huge national indebtedness. Paying interest on the debt then gives government leaders the excuse to impose more and more taxation. Another well-used tactic involves inviting — or forcing — massive numbers of citizens on to welfare rolls where they become dependent upon government. And still another calls for burdening the productive sector with costly, unnecessary and downright production-inhibiting regulations. The Bush administration is guilty of all of these socialism-building tactics even as the President dramatically boosts the world-government prospects of the United Nations.

Immediately after taking office in January 1989, President Bush unveiled a federal budget containing economic forecasts, as required by law, for several years into the future. On that occasion, the President's projections included $1,249 billion in spending for fiscal 1992 with a sharp decline in the deficit to $30.6 billion. His forecast for fiscal 1993 estimated spending at $1,284 billion with a *surplus* of $2.5 billion.

Three years later, in January 1992, the same President was forced to admit that the deficit for fiscal year 1992 (ending September 30, 1992) would top out at an estimated $399 billion, missing his earlier forecast by an astounding $368 billion! The deficit alone now exceeds the total federal budget during the height of the Vietnam War. He also announced that the 1991 fiscal year had been completed with a deficit of $267 billion.

In addition, his January 1992 forecast included a spending level of $1,520 billion for fiscal 1993 (up $236 billion from his 1989 projection) with a projected deficit of $352 billion instead of the modest surplus.

Most Americans remember the famous pledge given by candidate Bush in 1988. "Read my lips, no new taxes!" was the catchiest campaign slogan the nation had heard in many years. Yet, in October 1990, the President signed one of the largest tax increases in American history, $164 billion over five years. It was another body blow delivered to the nation's producers.

If any economic tinkering can help the nation out of a recession, it certainly isn't a tax increase. Yet, in the midst of the most severe economic slowdown since the great depression, the President cooperated in making it even worse by supporting the huge tax increase. A freshman economics student would tell you that you don't gobble up more consumer money with taxes when consumer spending is needed to spur economic recovery. But Mr. Bush helped the Insider cause with the harm done to economic vitality.

President Proposes Aid for Russia

Boris Yeltsin is currently the fair-haired hero of America's Insiders. Welcomed to New York City by David Rockefeller in September 1989, he was brought to CFR headquarters for a closed-door session presided over by the powerful former CFR chairman.[56] As one indication of Insider clout, the Russian leader went first to CFR headquarters and then to Washington to meet with President Bush.[57]

Eventually talking to reporters, Yeltsin lamented that "only one of the five classical components of socialism has been implemented — the nationalization of property." Yeltsin says he doesn't want a totally state-controlled economy, just 85 to 90 percent control. Let the people own 10 to 15 percent, he argues. Like his predecessor, Mikhail Gorbachev, he is a socialist through and through.[58]

The struggle for leadership in Russia between Mikhail Gorbachev and Boris Yeltsin has been won — at least temporarily — by Yeltsin. But the fight between these two has always been like the Insider-take-all struggles between George Bush (TC and CFR) and Michael Dukakis (CFR), or between Gerald Ford (CFR) and Jimmy Carter (TC), or between Richard Nixon (CFR) and Hubert Humphrey (CFR), or between Dwight Eisenhower (CFR) and Adlai Stevenson (CFR).[59] Each of these U.S. politicians willingly cooperated with the Insiders whose organizations they were happy to join. So too do Gorbachev and Yeltsin cooperate with the same Insiders.

Something else about the leaders of Russia needs to be said here. Both Gorbachev and Yeltsin are among the many former communists who share enormous guilt for the murder, terror and denial of basic human rights for millions in the former USSR and its captive nations. Both should be held accountable for their part in those crimes and for the slaughter of 1.4 million Afghan civilians during the 1980s. As members of the USSR's ruling Politburo during the incredibly cruel rape of Afghanistan, they are and should be classified arch-criminals. And if they are not, there is no such thing as an arch-criminal.

But President Bush — backed by the Insiders in government, the media, and elsewhere — is doing everything within his power to sustain such monsters in power. Promises of direct U.S. aid have been kept; commitments for more in the future have been given; and pledges of indirect aid from the International Monetary Fund have also been made. Early in 1992, Mr. Bush asked Congress to boost the U.S. commitment to IMF by $12 billion so that this organization could assist the socialists in Russia. He did so even while informing the nation that the U.S. government would, in that same year, add $400 billion more to its red ink totals.

Stopping the Insiders a Must

In the CFR's *Annual Report* for 1989, Peter Tarnoff, the organization's president, announced plans to create a larger office for the CFR in the nation's capital. Once built, he explained, the organization "will be better able to grow in Washington, and to attract many more Senate and House members and their staffs to our programs." CFR intentions to increase Insider influence over our nation's government were clearly enunciated.

On April 10, 1990, the *Wall Street Journal* published a small excerpt from a speech given by veteran CFR member Paul H. Nitze. The occasion for his remarks was the March 12th opening of that new Council on Foreign Relations office in Washington. Nitze described the great influence held by the "enormously important New York business and intellectual community," referring, of course, to CFR members who continue to reside in the New York area.

But while noting that Washington's importance within the CFR had grown dramatically, Nitze stated quite clearly exactly how the CFR had dominated U.S. policy from New York for 70 years. Beginning with a description of the Council's influence during the period of the 1920s and 1930s, he said:

> The State Department and White House might conduct diplomacy in peace and raise and command armies in war, but policy was made by serious people, men with a longer view, i.e. the great men of finance and their advisers. New York was where they were to be found.

Then, this veteran Insider from within the CFR, who has served in numerous administrations, added:

> In the postwar years, the Council has continued to represent an invaluable way for many of us Washingtonians to tap the enormously important New York business and intellectual community.[60]

In other words, national policy was set and continues to be set in New York — not by the elected leaders of this nation, but by members of "the Council." Over these years, national policy has included financing tyranny and destroying liberty all over the globe.[61] And President Bush has placed more CFR members in government posts than any predecessor. These Insiders, along with dozens of CFR members in the House and Senate,[62] plus those in New York who have not taken government posts but who retain great influence over national affairs, are leading this nation into the long-desired, tyrannical "new world order."

No American worthy of the name wants a "new world order." The world government sought by the architects of this new world order would mean an end to the nation we inherited, and the destruction of the greatest experiment in human liberty in the history of mankind. World government would also establish socialism in place of the free market system, a certain route to conversion of this nation into another Third World deadend. And, even worse, it would mean that tyranny had replaced liberty, a kind of tyranny that has been experienced by countless millions throughout the 20th century — a century of unparalleled barbarism created, sustained and favored by the Insiders of the most powerful conspiracy in the history of mankind.

The Insiders have taken us far down the various paths toward their satanically inspired goal. And time is running out if we are to save our nation and ourselves from their designs.

Real Americans who love their country and want to remain free don't have to lose this struggle. It can be won if enough seize the opportunity to take the U.S. government away from the Insiders and return it to individuals who believe in national independence and individual liberty, and who are not working to create the "new world order." And there is still time to thwart the plans of the Insiders and climb out of the tyrannical straitjacket they have prepared for us.

Understanding the domination of the Bush administration by the Insiders is an essential beginning step toward achieving victory over the whole rotten cabal. The enemy faced by Americans is a conspiracy, an organized group of Insiders seeking tyrannical control of this nation, and all nations. Its plans and its agents can be exposed and routed by an opposing force firmly rooted in principle and unwaveringly propelled by courage. The John Birch Society is such a force. Diligent adherence to the program of the Society by enough determined Americans is exactly what's needed to thwart the Insiders and to keep America free.

Your inquiry about how to get started on the climb back to full independence for our nation and economic freedom for yourself will be most welcome. We invite you to contact us without delay.

Notes

40. Rowland Evans and Robert Novak, "Bush and the Trilateral Commission," *St. Petersburg Times*, April 12, 1981.
41. Ron Rosenbaum, "The Last Secrets of Skull & Bones," *Esquire*, September 1977.
42. J. A. Engles, "U.N.Envoy Brash, Flexible," *Rochester* (NY) *Times-Union*, October 12, 1971.
43. United Press International dispatch from Peking, February 25, 1972.
44. Doyle McManus, "A New World Order: Bush's vision still fuzzy," *Milwaukee Journal*, February 24, 1991.
45. *Human Cost of Communism in China*, 1971 Report issued by the Senate Subcommittee to Investigate the Administration of the Internal Security Act and

Other Internal Security Laws.

46. *Annual Report 1972*, Council on Foreign Relations, 58 East 68th Street, New York, NY 10021.

47. "Membership List as of July 26, 1977," issued by The Trilateral Commission, 345 East 46th Street, New York, NY 10021.

48. *Annual Report 1978*, Council on Foreign Relations.

49. *Issues and Opinions: The Work Program of the Atlantic Council of the United States*, 1978, Atlantic Council, 1616 H Street NW, Washington, DC 20006.

50. News item, *Appleton* (WI) *Post-Crescent*, April 22, 1990.

51. G. Edward Griffin, *The Fearful Master* (Appleton, WI: Western Islands, 1964).

52. Alan Stang, *The Actor: The True Story of John Foster Dulles, Secretary of State, 1953-1959* (Appleton, WI: Western Islands, 1968). Mr. Stang's critical biography of John Foster Dulles supplies an excellent introduction to the conspiratorial view of history.

53. Robert W. Lee, *The United Nations Conspiracy* (Appleton, WI: Western Islands, 1981).

54. *Congressional Record*, January 10, 1991, Pages S106-S107. Senator Simon supplied constituents with copies of these pages of the CR containing his full statement to fellow senators.

55. Patrick J. Buchanan, "The Gulf Crisis Is the Last Hurrah of the Globalists," *Union Leader*, Manchester, NH, September 26, 1990.

56. *Annual Report 1990*, Council on Foreign Relations.

57. *Facts On File*, 1989, page 916.

58. A.M. Rosenthal, "Yeltsin fails to charm," *Milwaukee Journal*, September 21, 1989.

59. During the 1992 Presidential primaries, Democratic candidate Bill Clinton's membership in both the CFR and the TC never became an issue. Oppo-

nents Paul Tsongas, Jerry Brown, Tom Harkin, and Bob Kerrey were not themselves formal members of either of these Insider groups. Their refusal to make an issue out of Clinton's memberships, especially the fact that his ties to these organizations linked him to George Bush, can only mean that they would like to hold such memberships themselves and are not going to jeopardize the possibility of being invited to join either or both in the future.

60. "Notable & Quotable," *Wall Street Journal*, April 10, 1991. Four top leaders of the *Wall Street Journal* hold membership in the CFR: chairman & publisher Peter R. Kann; executive editor Norman Pearlstine; editor Robert L. Bartley; and managing editor Paul E. Steiger.

61. For a comprehensive and revealing history of the Council on Foreign Relations using its own source documents for evidence of its intentions to destroy national sovereignty and abolish personal freedom, see James Perloff's *The Shadows of Power*, 1988, Western Islands, Appleton, WI 54913.

62. As of June 30, 1991, the CFR *Annual Report 1991* lists the following U.S. Senators as CFR members: Boren (OK), Chafee (RI), Cohen (ME), Dodd (CT), Graham (FL), Lieberman (CT), Mitchell (ME), Moynihan (NY), Pell (RI), Pressler (SD), Robb (VA), Rockefeller (WV), Roth (DE), Rudman (NH), Sanford (NC), Wirth (CO), and Wofford (PA).

The following are some of the CFR members in the U.S. House of Representatives: Aspin (WI), Fascell (FL), Foley (WA), Gejdenson (CT), Gephardt (MO), Gingrich (GA), Houghton (NY), Johnson (CT), Levine (CA), McCurdy (OK), Moody (WI), Petri (WI), Schroeder (CO), Snowe (ME), Solarz (NY), Spratt (SC), Stokes (OH), and Wolpe (MI).

In April 1991, the Trilateral Commission listed

the following U.S. senators as members: Chafee (RI), Cohen (ME), Robb (VA), Rockefeller (WV), and Roth (DE).

And the TC listed the following U.S. representatives as members: Foley (WA), Leach (IA), and Rangel (NY).

Part IV — 1994

Democrat or Republican, it doesn't matter to the Insiders. Since at least the days of Franklin Roosevelt, they and their willing servants have dominated the leadership of both major political parties. Even if the occupant of the White House weren't himself a member of one or more of the Insider organizations, he was surrounded by those who were.

When the 1992 presidential sweepstakes began and George Bush was a sure bet to run for re-election, it was certain that the Democrats would select another Insider to oppose him. But early in the campaign, hardly anyone would have forecast that the choice would be Arkansas Governor Bill Clinton. True enough, Mr. Clinton should have been considered because of his own impressive list of Insider credentials. He was a member of both the Council on Foreign Relations and the Trilateral Commission, had attended the 1991 Bilderberg meeting at Baden-Baden in Germany, and had even spent two years at England's Oxford University in the Rhodes Scholar program.

But he hailed from a very small state, had no experience in foreign affairs, was merely in his mid-40s, and had made an absolutely dreadful impression in the only nationwide exposure he was ever given — his long, dry, and boring speech during the 1988 Democratic National Convention.

Evidently, none of these negatives mattered very much to the behind-the-scenes manipulators whose clout is critical in the selection of candidates. What they look for is someone willing to promote Insider goals. They know that powerfully placed Insiders in the mass media can, with relative ease, create almost any image whatsoever in the minds of the voting public. The main consideration for the Insiders has always been: Can we count on this man to carry our agenda forward?

Character, patriotism, religious values, personal integrity, family loyalty, honesty, and virtually all else that Americans hope to find in a chief executive count for nothing with Insiders. Those who know Mr. Clinton best know that he exhibits none of these important traits. Those who publish the only statewide newspaper in his home state, the *Arkansas Democrat Gazette*, know it too. Their blistering editorial refusing to support him for President stated, "It is not the compromises he has made that trouble so much as the unavoidable suspicion that he has no great principles to compromise."[63]

Media Ignore Damaging Information

Early in 1992, Bill Clinton was successfully rescued from the Gennifer Flowers incident, the draft-dodging incident, and the marijuana incident. He also survived his fawning appeals for support at gatherings of homosexual activists. It became perfectly obvious as the 1992 campaign heated up and none of these scandals drove Clinton out of the race that his was the candidacy favored by the Insider-controlled media.[64] Consider:

• In 1988, Colorado Senator Gary Hart's presidential aspirations hit the end of the road when his flirtations with a younger woman (not his wife) were reported in the press and on nationwide television. But Bill Clinton's sexual encounters with several women were swept aside after an initial flurry of notoriety. He even survived the public airing of his instructions to Gennifer Flowers about how to handle the press if questioned about their illicit relationship.[65]

• Conclusive evidence that Bill Clinton dishonorably dodged the draft came to light with the publication of his December 1969 letter[66] and a 1992 affidavit submitted by retired Colonel Eugene Holmes, the ROTC head at the University of Arkansas during the period when the future President was doing anything fair or foul to stay out of the military.[67] These letters, along with a great deal of additional evidence that surfaced and was eventually generally overlooked by the supposedly hard-nosed media, show that Bill Clinton a) used dishonorable means on several occasions to evade the draft; b) likely committed a felony in the process; and c) repeatedly lied about what he had done.

In his 1969 letter to Colonel Holmes, young Mr. Clinton actually expressed his "loathing for the military," an attitude shared to this day by many of the 1960s-style anti-war activists he has placed in government posts.[68]

• After having denied on numerous occasions that he had ever smoked marijuana, Mr. Clinton admitted on the MTV television network during the campaign that he had done so and would do it again.[69] In 1987, U.S. Appeals Court Judge Douglas H. Ginsburg was forced to withdraw his name for consideration as a Supreme Court justice when he admitted that he had smoked marijuana on a few occasions many years before. He had obviously committed a crime at the time and was deemed unfit to sit on the Supreme Court. But the media let Clinton's admission pass as if nothing had happened.

• During the 1992 campaign, Bill Clinton eagerly sought and certainly received the active support of the homosexual movement.[70] In return for this support, he promised to lift the military's ban on their "lifestyle." On November 11, 1992, a mere eight days after the votes had been counted, the President-elect's first policy statement outlined his plan to keep the promise he made to the homosexuals. He later ran into a buzzsaw of opposition and was forced to back off, but only partially.[71]

All of these sides of Bill Clinton were again brought to public attention four months after the inauguration when, during a formal speech before U.S. Air Force personnel in Europe, a two-star general labeled the new President a "pot smoking ... gay-loving ... draft-dodging ... and womanizing" commander in chief during a formal speech.[72] After high military officials investigated the incident, Air Force Major General Harold N. Campbell was fined, demoted, and forced to retire. The horror, however, isn't that a senior military officer showed any disrespect for the President, or that he was sternly disciplined; the horror is that everything he said was completely true.

• In late May 1994, President Clinton chose to award Congressional Medals of Honor to the families of two American soldiers killed during 1992's bungled military action in Somalia. Mr. Herbert Shugart, the father of an Army sergeant who died rescuing a downed helicopter pilot, refused to shake the President's hand. The still-grieving man told Mr. Clinton: "You are not fit to be President of the United States. The blame for my son's death rests with the White House and you. You are not fit to command."

Though a bevy of American newsmen witnessed

this startling rebuff, our nation's Insider-dominated media refused to report it anywhere in the United States. Details did appear, however, in the May 29, 1994 issue of England's *Sunday London Times*. Two weeks later, columnist Richard Grenier reported both the incident and the "amazing" absence of any American coverage.[73]

Favoritism Draws Protest

Do we overstate the media's protection of Bill Clinton? Not really, because the favoritism even drew comments from sources friendly to the President. Columnist Philip Terzian, for instance, has spent a career close to the Insiders. He served for a time as a speechwriter for former Secretary of State and CFR heavyweight Cyrus Vance. But less than six weeks before the 1992 election, he became so incensed about the pro-Clinton bias of his media colleagues that he wrote:

> If Clinton has been harassed by the press on the subject of Gennifer Flowers, or his variable descriptions of his military career, it has escaped my attention.... You can imagine the reaction if George Bush's purported mistress furnished tapes of their naughty chit-chat. Or if witnesses persisted in contradicting his stories about national service. And that is precisely the problem. For the most part, journalistic bias against Bush, and in favor of Clinton, is so obvious, so pervasive, so natural to the press corps, that it is scarcely worth noticing.[74]

Why did so many elements of the mass media ignore or sweep aside Bill Clinton's clouded record and go to work for him? Why was his reprehensible personal conduct downplayed? Part of the answer is that most political reporters, if pressed, admit to harboring Clinton-style left-of-center views. But some media luminaries, especially Insiders in top management positions, were likely motivated by a deeper and more sinister ambition. Namely, by focusing some attention on Clinton's moral deficiencies, and then sweeping everything about them under a rug while sweeping him into the White House, these luminaries could help sink national morality even lower.

If a known philanderer, liar, drug user, and cheerleader for the homosexual lifestyle can be elected President of the United States, then lying, philandering, drug use, and acceptance of homosexual activity are boosted. The combined increase in acceptability of these forms of immorality is surely as deadly an attack on the moral fabric of America as can be imagined.

Aspiring to Be an Insider

Bill Clinton publicly stated his aspirations for high political office as a teenager. While studying international affairs at Georgetown University (1964-68), he became a disciple of Professor Carroll Quigley. A Harvard-trained historian, Quigley's monumental *Tragedy and Hope: A History of the World In Our Time* was published in 1966.[75] Mr. Clinton either read this 1,348-page book or was exposed to its message by Quigley in person. On July 16, 1992, right in the middle of his triumphant speech accepting the Democratic Party's nomination for President, he threw a verbal bouquet to "a professor I had named Carroll Quigley." If most of the vast television audience wondered who Quigley was, both the Insiders and those who study them and their goals knew immediately.

In his book, Quigley described in great detail the creation of a "secret society" for world rule hatched at England's Oxford University in the late 1800s. As spelled out with enthusiasm by Quigley, the Cecil Rhodes-led group sought "nothing less than to create a world system of financial control in private hands able to dominate the political system of each country and the economy of the world as a whole."[76] The fabulously wealthy Rhodes bankrolled much of the group's efforts and later launched the Rhodes Scholar program described by Quigley in another of his books as "merely a facade to conceal the secret society."[77]

Quigley related that a key accomplishment of this secret society was the creation of "Institutes of International Affairs in the British dominion nations and in the United States (where it is known as the Council on Foreign Relations)...."[78] In 1973, top leaders of the CFR at the time, including chairman David Rockefeller and Columbia University professor Zbigniew Brzezinski, launched the Trilateral Commission.

Introduced to the world of the "secret society" by Quigley, Bill Clinton successfully sought acceptance as a Rhodes Scholar. He spent two years in the program (1968-70), some of it organizing protests throughout Europe against America's military and the U.S. effort in Vietnam — even while it was raging!

The future President spent so much time in anti-war activities that he never finished his studies at Oxford, and he returned to the U.S. in 1970 to attend Yale University's law school. While at

Yale, he shared an apartment with Hillary Rodham and eventually married her in 1975.

From Yale, he went back to Arkansas and in only a few years won election as that state's Attorney General and then Governor. In 1988, he was tapped for membership in the CFR.[79] One year later, he was welcomed into membership in the Trilateral Commission.[80]

Then, in 1991, he journeyed to Baden-Baden in Germany to attend the annual meeting of the Bilderbergers, a group of world government promoters formed by David Rockefeller and Prince Bernhard of the Netherlands at the Hotel de Bilderberg in Oosterbeek, Holland in 1954. Three-day Bilderberg conferences, attended by many of the top leaders of the Western world, are always held at a plush resort amidst deep secrecy. Bernhard actually confirmed the anti-sovereignty and internationalist agenda of the group in his authorized biography.[81]

These Insider credentials weren't unknown to Mr. Clinton's opponents during the 1992 Democratic nomination process. But with the single exception of a slight mention by former California Governor Jerry Brown, none of these challengers made an issue of them.

Democratic challengers Paul Tsongas, Bob Kerrey, Tom Harkin, Jesse Jackson, and Douglas Wilder could have pointed to the similar pedigrees of Bill Clinton and George Bush, both of whom had ties to the CFR, TC and Bilderbergers. But this golden issue went begging for attention. Tsongas, who soon joined with CFR chairman Peter G. Peterson in the Concord Coalition, wasn't about to attack the group led by his patron-to-be. The others, most likely looking for invitations to join some or all of these groups, submitted to the unwritten rule which forbids focusing attention on any element of Insider power.

Clinton Wins With 43 Percent

The mass media told Americans that the election of 1992 produced a victory for the Democrats — and it did. But the real winners, once again, were the Insiders. With their help, William Jefferson Clinton won the prize with only 43 percent of the popular vote in a three-man race (George Bush garnered 38 percent and Ross Perot walked away with 19 percent). With 370 electoral votes to Mr. Bush's 168, the Arkansas governor became the 42nd President of our nation.

Analysts will never cease offering opinions about the Perot factor in the 1992 race. But few will even mention the highly interesting item seen on the front page of the *Wall Street Journal* on May 29, 1992. Here it is exactly as it appeared:

> **FRIEND IN NEED:** Perot's candidacy for the prestigious Council on Foreign Relations several years ago was seconded by ... George Bush. A Perot aide says Bush's letter was "lovely," but that there aren't any plans to release the text.[82]

If former CFR board member George Bush felt Ross Perot was a worthy candidate for CFR membership, then Ross Perot's 1992 candidacy offered nothing substantial in the way of change. Mr. Bush simply would not give such an endorsement to an enemy of the Insiders. As it turned out, Perot's presence in the race surely drew a great many votes away from George Bush. And the

Bush re-election effort was widely described as the most poorly run presidential campaign in U.S. political history. Whether he knew it or not, Perot's candidacy figured mightily in the victory for Bill Clinton, the first choice of the Insiders.

CFR Advises, Clinton Acts

CFR leaders devoted their entire Winter 1992/1993 issue of *Foreign Affairs* to "Advice For President Clinton." Though published shortly after the November election, much of it was obviously written prior to Election Day because references to "candidate" Clinton appear throughout. Even if CFR leaders didn't know for certain that Bill Clinton would win, the "advice" they gave could just as easily have been given to George Bush — with just as much expectation that it would be followed.

What follows are distillations of numerous portions of the CFR's "advice," followed by evidence of Bill Clinton's willingness to accept and implement it.

CFR member Leon V. Sigal thought additional aid for Boris Yeltsin was needed. He also recommended more foreign aid across the board, passage of the North American Free Trade Agreement (NAFTA), and keeping U.S. troops in Europe.

Yeltsin got more aid; more money taken from the American people is flowing to the four corners of the earth even while deficits and debt pile up here at home; U.S. troops are still in Europe (and elsewhere); and the President put every ounce of his energy into arm-twisting Congress to approve

NAFTA.

NAFTA creates an economic union among Mexico, Canada and the U.S., a step paving the way for political union — a favored route to world government. Predictably, one after another of the Insiders' big guns fired off salvos urging its passage. In his syndicated column, CFR and TC guru Henry Kissinger branded NAFTA "the most creative step toward a new world order" in the past 50 years.[83] Not to be outdone, CFR chairman emeritus and TC founder David Rockefeller labeled any opposition to NAFTA "criminal."[84] Bill Clinton's enthusiasm for NAFTA was hardly surprising.

CFR member Jeffrey E. Garten, an employee of CFR chairman Peter G. Peterson at the New York-based Blackstone Group investment banking firm, urged the new President to launch more job-training programs, raise taxes, work for "interdependence" instead of independence, increase economic ties to Japan and Germany, and approve both NAFTA and GATT (the General Agreement on Tariffs and Trade).

In March 1994, President Clinton hosted a meeting in Detroit where 176 of the G-7 leaders dined in royal splendor and pontificated about the world's unemployment problems. The last thing on their minds was leaving money in the hands of beleaguered taxpayers, the people who create jobs. Mr. Clinton had already reneged on his solemn campaign pledge to cut taxes for the middle class and, instead, pushed through a huge tax increase. After the Detroit meeting, he journeyed to

Seattle to meet with delegates from Japan and other Asian nations to work for formation of an Asia-Pacific economic union. In mid-November 1994, he journeyed to Indonesia to meet with Asian leaders for the same purpose. And, exactly as he was urged, he began using all the power of his office to promote passage of GATT.

CFR member Michael S. Teitelbaum advised the newly elected President to use taxpayers' money to expand America's role in controlling world population.

Mr. Clinton sent former Colorado Senator Timothy Wirth (CFR), an avid pro-abortionist and population controller, to lead the U.S. delegation at the UN's September 1994 International Conference on Population and Development held in Cairo, Egypt. In addition to its many criticisms of U.S. government involvement in the field of population, the International Right To Life Federation has accurately labeled this joint UN and Clinton administration venture as "pro-abortion imperialism."

CFR member General Colin Powell enthusiastically called for more use of America's military for UN-directed "peacekeeping and humanitarian operations" and for continued use of the force of arms "to achieve our political objectives."

General Powell was one of 40 CFR favorites whose photo appeared on the cover of the CFR's *Annual Report* for 1990. As further evidence of his intimacy with the CFR, he gathered the leaders of each of our nation's military services for an April 22, 1993 meeting with the CFR's Foreign Policy Roundtable group in his office at the Pentagon.[85] He was a likely choice to provide CFR advice to the incoming President.

On May 3, 1994, President Clinton signed Presidential Decision Directive 25 (PDD-25) outlining new roles for our nation's military in the area of international "peacekeeping." The text of this important document was immediately classified, but an official "summary" was released by the office of National Security Adviser Anthony Lake. It states that American military personnel — each of whom joined the military of this nation, not the UN's military — can be assigned to the UN for its response to "territorial disputes, armed ethnic conflicts, civil wars (many of which could spill across international borders), and the collapse of government authority in some states...." In other words, the U.S. military is to be the UN's globocop for virtually any assignment the UN chooses. Such a policy constitutes an immense betrayal of our uniformed services.[86]

In keeping with the recommendations given by Powell in *Foreign Affairs*, and acting in accord with the unconstitutional provisions of PDD-25 given in the summary, Mr. Clinton sent tens of thousands of U.S. troops in September 1994 into Haiti "to enforce the UN resolutions" addressing that nation's domestic turmoil. Once there, the troops were assigned the task of disarming the civilian population and changing the nation's leaders. And only several weeks later, the President sent more tens of thousands of troops back into Kuwait, again "to enforce UN resolutions" addressing Saddam Hussein's expansionist aims.

Under Mr. Clinton's watch, America's military is fast becoming the UN's dutiful servant.

Trilateral Commission veteran Barber B. Conable and CFR member David M. Lampton co-authored an article urging Mr. Clinton to overlook China's abysmal human rights record and "build links to the most dynamic regional economy in the world." These two Insiders chided Mr. Clinton for his campaign pledge not to renew Most Favored Nation trade status for China unless definite progress on the human rights front had been documented.

During the 1992 election, candidate Clinton berated President Bush for "coddling" the tyrants who rule Communist China. Once in office, he gave the Chinese rulers another year to demonstrate progress regarding human rights or face stiff new trade regulations. China did nothing to change its loathsome disregard for elementary rights. Nevertheless, in June 1994, the President not only renewed Most Favored Nation status for China, but he permanently removed consideration of China's human rights policies from any future extension of MFN status. This means that U.S. taxpayers will supply more loans, subsidies, and technology transfers to sustain a government that presides over a nation that is history's largest concentration camp.

Although we have only cited a few examples demonstrating that some of the CFR's "advice" has been followed by the President, CFR leaders have every reason to believe they can count on Bill Clinton for whatever they want. His compliance with Insider wishes and his many appointments of Insiders to high government posts indicate very clearly whose agenda he follows.

Clinton Appointments

Not surprisingly, most of the Clinton administration's top appointees have CFR and/or TC credentials. The most important post, Secretary of State, was given to Warren Christopher, a CFR board member during the 1980s, the CFR's vice chairman from 1988 until he resigned to accept the Clinton appointment, and a member of the TC from its launching in 1973. Christopher served as Deputy Secretary of State during the Carter administration where he used his position to pressure the Senate to give the U.S. Canal in Panama to the communist-dominated Torrijos regime. He then worked to force the Shah out of Iran and Somoza out of Nicaragua. Ayatollah Khomeini and the communist Sandinistas were most grateful.

R. James Woolsey (CFR and Rhodes) was appointed CIA Director; Madeleine Albright (CFR) was named U.S. Ambassador to the UN; and W. Anthony Lake (CFR) accepted the post of National Security Advisor. Former Wisconsin Congressman Les Aspin (CFR) served as Secretary of Defense until he was ushered out in less than a year. Mr. Clinton immediately offered the post to retired Admiral Bobby Ray Inman (CFR), who had succeeded Warren Christopher as vice chairman of the CFR. For reasons still unclear, Inman first accepted and then declined the post. The post was then awarded to William J. Perry, who, even though he supports the pro-UN positions of the CFR/TC,[87] remains one of very few top appointees who has not yet achieved CFR or TC membership.

For Secretary of the Treasury, Clinton chose Texas Senator Lloyd Bentsen, a CFR member during the 1980s. When Bentsen stepped down after two years, the job went to New York financier and CFR member Robert E. Rubin. Former University of Wisconsin chancellor Donna Shalala (CFR and TC) now serves as Secretary of Health and Human Services; former Arizona Governor Bruce Babbitt (CFR and TC) is Secretary of the Interior; former San Antonio Mayor Henry Cisneros (CFR and TC) is Secretary of Housing and Urban Development; Alice Rivlin (CFR and TC) began service on the Clinton team as deputy director of the Office of Management and Budget and became its Director when Leon Panetta moved to a White House post.

When President Clinton needed a good public relations expert for the White House, he turned to David Gergen (CFR and TC) and steered George Stephanopoulos (CFR and Rhodes) into another White House post. Gergen was later sent to the State Department, where public relations expertise was deemed lacking. Needing someone to serve as ambassador to Trilateralist Japan, the President tapped former Vice President Walter Mondale (CFR and TC). And for Ambassador to Spain, Mr. Clinton turned to Richard N. Gardner (CFR and TC), whose treasonous urging for "an end run around national sovereignty, eroding it piece by piece" remains the most concise statement of Insider designs.[88]

Where the CFR's *Annual Report* for 1992 reported that 387 of the organization's members were U.S. government officials, the 1993 *Annual Report* curiously departed from its longstanding practice of supplying such breakdowns. But the

1994 *Annual Report* noted that 463 members of the CFR (15 percent of the 3,136 members) were serving as "U.S. government officials," the highest number during any administration.

Social and Political Revolutionaries

During his 14-minute Inaugural Address, Mr. Clinton managed to use the word "change" eight times. In one passage, he said there was a need to "reinvent America" and that "each generation must define what it means to be an American."

But the Americanism given us by our nation's Founding Fathers is the most praiseworthy system in all history. *It doesn't need change; it needs restoration.* A President loyal to America's fundamental principles would do all in his power to champion a return to government limited by law (the Constitution) and to a people limited by freely accepted moral codes (e.g., the Ten Commandments). Bill Clinton continues to work for the exact opposite.

Appearing on the MTV program "Enough Is Enough" on April 19, 1994, Mr. Clinton turned the American system further on its head with his claim that the "radical Constitution" and the "radical Bill of Rights" were responsible for "giving a radical amount of individual freedom to Americans." With that statement, he indicated his belief that rights are not God-given, as clearly stated in the Declaration of Independence, but government-given. Of course, the President can hardly be unaware that whatever a government can give, it can also take away. His appointment of social and political revolutionaries, therefore, is hardly surprising.

During the same MTV interview, Mr. Clinton

uttered the following revolutionary statement: "When personal freedom's being abused, you have to move to limit it. That's what we did in the announcement I made last weekend on the public housing projects, about how we're going to have weapons sweeps and more things like that...."[89] In other words, forget the prohibition against unwarranted searches noted in the Fourth Amendment; government can do whatever it likes.

The drive to have homosexuality made socially acceptable received a tremendous boost when Mr. Clinton invited national leaders of the movement into the White House on April 16, 1993. He not only posed for photographs with them but he went out of his way in supplying "tips" about how to present their cause to the press and the nation. He had already named several known homosexuals to federal positions. Bob Hattoy, an openly avowed homosexual who was a featured speaker at the Democratic Party's 1992 convention, not only brought a militant attitude about his "lifestyle" to his post as an associate director of personnel in the White House. He also brought his own case of AIDS.

In June 1994, the extent of the administration's pro-homosexual bias was graphically illustrated by the forced reassignment of Dr. Karl Mertz, a senior official in the Department of Agriculture. While enjoying a vacation earlier in the year, Mertz had been a guest on a Mississippi television program. Asked what he thought of proposals within his department to provide homosexual employees with the same benefits supplied to legally married heterosexual employees, he said: "I am speaking as a Christian; I'm not speaking for the USDA. We need to be moving toward Camelot, not Sodom and Gomorrah, and I'm afraid that's where our leadership is trying to take us." In short order, he was reassigned to a new job about which he has stated: "I am wasting the taxpayer's money. I am in a job that is unnecessary."[90]

The President found an extremely vocal and militant homosexual in San Francisco city official Roberta Achtenberg. Named as an assistant secretary in the Department of Housing and Urban Development, she faced strong opposition during Senate confirmation hearings because of her crusade to terminate United Way funding for the Boy Scouts. She targeted the Scouts for refusing to allow homosexual leaders and for retaining the reference to God in the Scout Oath.

For the top civil rights post in the attorney general's office, Mr. Clinton nominated his wife's close friend, University of Pennsylvania law professor Lani Guinier. An "expert" on voting rights laws, she favors "proportional representation" by race. A black herself, she has proposed "granting blacks a minority veto" over a wide array of legislation, investing them with more than equal opportunity, and assisting them to gain political power as a bloc by doing away with representation by population and substituting "proportionate interest representation." When a storm of protest arose over her incredibly racist and unconstitutional views, the President was forced to withdraw her name.

The President's first Surgeon General, Dr. Joycelyn Elders, managed to win Senate approval despite her own frontal assault on traditional family and moral values. Elders, who served under Governor Clinton in Arkansas, has long distinguished herself as a combative proponent of compulsory sex education for children from kindergarten through high school, abortion rights, and contraceptive distribution — all at taxpayer expense. She favors studying the legalization of narcotics, and holds that girls should take contraceptives along when they go on dates.

On June 20, 1994, 87 members of the U.S. House signed a letter to President Clinton urging that Dr. Elders be fired. The letter stated in part, "She should be using this office to fight sickness and disease and not using this office to fight parents and churches."[91] Her response to the House members came in a New York speech delivered to the Lesbian and Gay Health Conference on June 22nd in which she attacked those who disagree as follows: "We've got to be strong to take on those people who are selling our children out in the name of religion."[92]

Finally, when she publicly suggested that masturbation should be taught in the schools, the President reluctantly asked for her resignation.

Mrs. Clinton and Vice President Gore

Any survey of the revolutionary intentions of the President must include the views of his activist spouse. A crusader for the alleged rights of children at the expense of parental prerogatives, Hillary Rodham Clinton has long favored massive expansion of federal child-care programs and a radical redefinition of the relationship between parents and their children. Perhaps the most bizarre of her yearnings is her hope to do away with any legal presumption of the commonality of interests between parents and their children, even to inserting a judge as the arbiter in any dispute between parents and a teenager.[93]

Appointed chairman of the leftist Legal Services Corporation during the Carter administration, she intensified that organization's advocacy for liberal causes, even illegally diverting LSC funds to political campaigns and causes.[94] As chairman of the New World Foundation, she helped to funnel money to an array of far left groups[95] including CISPES (the fund-raising arm for the communist FMLN in El Salvador), and the National Lawyers Guild, the longtime legal bulwark of the Communist Party USA.[96]

Spearheading the administration's drive to socialize American medicine, she exhibited her total disdain for free enterprise while briefing a congressional panel in July 1993. Asked if she understood that her proposal for forcing employers to finance employee health care would financially ruin many small- and medium-sized businesses, she responded, "I cannot be responsible for saving every undercapitalized entrepreneur in America."[97]

Nor should the hard-left leanings of Albert Gore, Jr. be ignored. Insiders who favor more government on the way to total government were surely delighted when the Tennessee senator was selected as Bill Clinton's running mate. With his liberal voting record second only to that of ultraleftist Senator Alan Cranston (D-CA),[98] Gore rarely met an increase in taxes or controls he didn't champion. His performance in the Senate placed him beyond Senator Ted Kennedy (D-MA) in left field.

Already well known for far-out views, Gore became renowned in liberal circles through the publication of his book *Earth in the Balance*.[99] Full of unsubstantiated rumors and wild claims offered as scientific facts, the book proceeds to recommend grandiose schemes for massive new government controls over people and industry.

Earth in the Balance urges readers to participate in "a bold effort to change the very foundation of our civilization." That parallels Bill Clinton's Inaugural Address urging fundamental change. Toward the end of his book, Gore labels automobile emissions "a mortal threat ... more deadly than that of any military enemy we are ever again likely to confront." He recommends "completely eliminating the internal combustion engine" over a period of 25 years! If he has his way, it's goodbye automobile and a great many other engine-driven machines.

Confirming our own analysis of this dangerous radical, former Washington Governor Dixy Lee Ray, a trained scientist with impressive credentials, sharply criticized Gore's bogus science in her book, *Environmental Overkill*.[100] She took him to task for wanting population controls, technology transfers to Third World nations, a huge new bureaucracy enforcing regulatory powers, international pacts able to skirt limitations in the Constitution, and his extensive scheme to brainwash the public about the environment.

Dangerous Supreme Court Choices

In 1971, an article about the CFR appearing in a major American newspaper provided a rare look inside the group. Written by Anthony Lukas, it stated in part:

> Everyone knows how fraternity brothers can help other brothers climb the ladder of life. If you want to make foreign policy,

there's no better fraternity to belong to than the Council.

When Henry Stimson — the group's quintessential member — went to Washington in 1940 as Secretary of War, he took with him John McCloy, who was to become Assistant Secretary in charge of personnel. McCloy has recalled: "Whenever we needed a man we thumbed through the roll of the Council members and put through a call to New York."

And over the years, the men McCloy called in turn called other Council members.[101]

As we have already demonstrated, Bill Clinton has enthusiastically followed the CFR's practice of having its members place other CFR members in executive branch posts. But he has also named CFR members to the judicial branch of government. At his first opportunity to place someone on the Supreme Court, he chose DC Appeals Court Justice Ruth Bader Ginsburg, whose membership in the CFR dates back to the mid-1970s. For his second nominee, the President tapped Boston-based Appeals Court Justice Stephen Breyer whose affiliation with the CFR began in the early 1980s.

While membership in the CFR is not a completely conclusive indicator of commitment to Insider goals, these two judges share a common attitude about government control of all education. In her 1981 ruling in *Wright v. Regan* for the DC Court of Appeals, Ginsburg ordered the IRS to impose harsh "affirmative action" racial quotas on the nation's private schools. Her decision to force these schools to recruit minority students and faculty was such a blatant violation of the

First Amendment that it was later overturned by the Supreme Court. [102]

In his 1989 decision in *New Life Baptist Church v. East Longmeadow School District* for the First District Court of Appeals, Breyer ruled that a private religious school must follow government regulations regarding selection of teachers, curriculum, and teaching methodology. Deemed "extraordinarily dangerous" by religious and home-school advocates, this decision prompted Michael Farris, president of Home School Legal Defense Association, to claim that Judge Breyer should "be viewed as totalitarian." [103]

Destroying Checks and Balances

With the arrival of Ginsburg and Breyer, there are now three CFR members serving on the high court. (Judge Sandra Day O'Connor was named to the CFR in 1991, several years after she took her place on the Supreme Court.) This means that three out of the nine members of our nation's highest court are formally allied with this numerically small (3,136 members) but extremely potent citadel of Insider power.

We have already detailed the overwhelming dominance of the executive branch by CFR members — from the Presidency and the various cabinet posts to a host of other important positions. Turning to the legislative branch, we find the most powerful posts in each House have been held for several years by CFR members George Mitchell (D-ME), Senate Majority Leader; Thomas Foley (D-WA), Speaker of the House; Richard Gephardt (D-MO), House Majority Leader; and Newt Gingrich (R-GA), Minority Whip, the second highest Republican post in the House. [104] After the

Republican victories in the 1994 elections, CFR member Gingrich became House Speaker and CFR member Gephardt became House Minority Leader.

Any student of the American system knows that the U.S. Constitution includes a system of checks and balances. Each branch of government is supposed to be a jealous guardian of its own prerogatives and a watchdog over the ambitions of the other branches. But if a single organization has enormous clout over all three, as the CFR clearly does, the whole system of checks and balances can be negated.

In his commentary on the importance of separating the various powers of government, James Madison stated: "The accumulation of all powers, legislative, executive, and judiciary, in the same hands ... may justly be pronounced the very definition of tyranny."[105] Impressive Insider influence in each branch of government is leading this nation toward the very tyranny the Father of the Constitution warned about.

Leaders of the U.S. government routinely operate as if they are empowered to do anything favored by a majority in Congress, or anything not specifically prohibited in the body of the Constitution. Such thinking is completely backwards and totally subversive. The federal government is supposed to be limited to only those powers *specifically authorized by the Constitution*.

The Constitution's very first sentence states that all legislative powers "herein granted" are vested in the Congress. The document later lists the very few powers that were granted to the federal government. But Congress has assumed a vast array of powers not granted, and the Supreme Court has so often made law through judicial fiat that the American people regularly treat its decisions as "the law of the land." Of course, the fundamental principle we are pointing to was reinforced with the Tenth Amendment.[106]

There is no authorization in the Constitution — to which all government leaders have sworn loyalty — for a long list of federal activities that are building government power, bleeding the people of their wealth, and guiding the nation into totalitarian control. Bill Clinton has spent great amounts of energy twisting congressional arms for such extra-constitutional programs as foreign aid, gun controls, federal aid for and eventual control of local police, more international entanglements, and programs dealing with education, agriculture, medicine, housing, and a host of other fields where federal power is enormous — and growing.

If the path down which America is being taken is not changed and the Constitution not restored to full force and effect, the American people will soon find themselves trapped in a duplicate of the worst communist dictatorship ever experienced. Its force and brutality, however, will not be generated from Moscow, or Beijing, or Havana — but from Washington, DC. And anyone who refuses to bow to federal dictates will face the full force of federal power, even the force of guns, tanks, and planes similar to those unleashed in March 1993 on the Branch Davidians in Waco, Texas.

CFR Protests Disingenuous

Anyone who contacts the CFR to ask about its commanding grip on our nation will be informed that the organization is merely a debating society, takes no positions on issues, and is open to all views. CFR chairman Peter G. Peterson and other Council members repeatedly state as much in published statements and responses to inquiries. But the CFR chairman also stated in his "Letter From the Chairman" in the CFR's 1989 *Annual Report* that "the Board of Directors and the staff of the Council have decided that this institution should play a leadership role in defining these new foreign policy agenda...."

How, we ask, can an organization define the foreign policy agenda for the United States without taking a position? Obviously, it can't. And any CFR claim that it takes no position on issues is a lie.

In a revealing op-ed column appearing in the October 30, 1993 *Washington Post*, staff writer Richard Harwood described the membership of the CFR as "the nearest thing we have to a ruling class in the United States." Never condemning the CFR's domination of the government and mass media even while he demonstrated the enormous clout of its members name-by-name and position-by-position, Harwood wrote of these powerfully placed Insiders:

> They do not merely analyze and interpret foreign policy for the United States; they help make it.[107]

He clearly does not agree that the CFR is merely a debating society open to all views. Many who are not among the CFR elite want the U.S. to withdraw from the United Nations, terminate all foreign aid, bring our military forces home, adhere strictly to the intent of the Constitution, cancel all entangling alliances, and mind our own business. But such views fall outside the CFR's "agenda" and are labeled "extreme" or "ultra" and given little or no respect by Insider trend setters.

What Americans Must Do

Believers in the American traditions of limited government and responsible citizenship must begin to take our government and our institutions back. Voting Americans took a sizable step in this direction when they repudiated the Clinton style of leadership and elected a new Congress in 1994. Even dazed left-wingers in the media had to admit that the dramatic shift amounted to a demand for a less intrusive government and a return to traditional values.[108] Other analysts found themselves unable to face the fact that the American people are becoming aware of the revolutionary programs being promoted by Mr. Clinton and his Insider mentors.

But, even with the welcome 1994 election results, totalitarian-minded Insiders still control most of what happens in our nation. The arrival in Congress of more Republicans, many of whom claim to be conservatives and opponents of internationalism, amounts only to a modest shift toward constitutional government that could be reversed in the next congressional elections. In addition, the newly arrived House and Senate members face numerous types of pressure to conform to the Insider-set agenda — from the leftist national media, from House Speaker Gingrich (a CFR member), and from lobbyists and special-interest proponents who frequently gain far more influence with a member of Congress than that possessed by his constituents.

There is no substitute for public awareness about the designs of the Insiders and about who is doing their bidding. No one who cares about the future should relax and expect that the job of retaking government was accomplished in 1994.

The Insiders and their plans must be exposed and cast aside. How to do it, you wonder? Your best move is to contact The John Birch Society. You will be provided information outlining a proven program put together by experienced leaders who know and love America, and who also know and despise the tyranny planned for all of us.

The stakes are nothing short of a future marked by national independence and personal liberty. If you won't mind living as a slave under a tyrannical world government, do nothing. But if you value freedom and opportunity for yourself and your family, join The John Birch Society and begin to lead others to do the same.

Time is running out. Don't delay. What will happen to our nation and our way of life if the Insiders are not exposed and repudiated is simply unthinkable.

Notes

63. *Arkansas Democrat Gazette*, October 28, 1992.
64. CFR members can be found at the top of ABC, CBS, NBC, CNN, *Time, Newsweek, U.S. News & World Report, National Review, New York Times, Washington Post, Wall Street Journal, Los Angeles Times*, and elsewhere in the nation's premier news-dispensing arena. The CFR *Annual Report 1994* notes that 330 (or 11 percent) of this organization's members are "Journalists, correspon-

dents & communications executives."

65. Portions of several September – December 1991 telephone conversations between Bill Clinton and Gennifer Flowers, including then-Governor Clinton's recommendations about how to handle media questions about their relationship, were placed in the *Congressional Record* on September 23, 1992 (pp. H 9262-65) by Rep. Robert Dornan (R-CA).

66. *Congressional Record*, July 30, 1992, pp. H 7051-52.

67. *Congressional Record*, September 17, 1992, p. H 8720.

68. For a more complete report on the incredible draft-dodging, anti-American, and pro-Vietcong activism of Mr. Clinton, see William F. Jasper, "Whom Have We Elected?" *The New American*, February 22, 1993, pp. 21-27.

69. Mr. Clinton's response on the June 16, 1992 MTV program when asked if he would ever inhale marijuana was, "Sure, if I could. I tried before."

70. The May 20, 1992 issue of *USA Today* reported Mr. Clinton's appearance at a gathering of homosexuals as follows: "For the first time ... the presumptive nominee of a major political party openly appealed for homosexual support. 'What I came here today to tell you in simple terms is, I have a vision and you're part of it.'"

71. The eventual adoption of the "Don't ask; don't tell, don't pursue" policy by the military didn't give homosexuals everything they wanted but it was a resounding victory for those who have adopted this "lifestyle." And it has had an extremely harmful and demoralizing effect on our nation's military personnel.

72. John Lancaster, "Accused of Ridiculing Clinton,

General Faces Air Force Probe," *Washington Post*, June 8, 1994.

73. Richard Grenier, "The end of the rugged individualists?", *Washington Times*, June 15, 1994.

74. Philip Terzian, "The Public vs. The Press: If only journalists would grow up," *Atlanta Constitution*, September 23, 1992.

75. Carroll Quigley, *Tragedy and Hope* (New York: Macmillan Company, 1966).

76. Ibid. p. 324.

77. Carroll Quigley, *The Anglo-American Establishment* (New York: Books In Focus, Inc., 1981).

78. *Tragedy and Hope*, op. cit., p. 132.

79. *Annual Report 1989*, The Council on Foreign Relations, New York.

80. Membership List, April 3, 1989; published by The Trilateral Commission, New York.

81. Alden Hatch, *Bernhard, Prince of the Netherlands* (New York: Doubleday, 1962).

82. *Wall Street Journal*, May 29,1992.

83. Henry Kissinger, "NAFTA: Clinton's Defining Task," *Washington Post*, July 20, 1993.

84. David Rockefeller, "A Hemisphere in the Balance," *Wall Street Journal*, October 1, 1994.

85. *Annual Report 1993*, The Council on Foreign Relations, New York, p. 76.

86. John F. McManus, "Sovereignty Sellout," *The New American*, July 11, 1994.

87. See William J. Perry, Ashton Carter and John Steinbruner, "A New Concept of Cooperative Security," Brookings Institution monograph, 1992: "Some of the ground and air forces that are in excess of national requirements could be configured for use in a multinational military force that could enforce U.N. sanctions when necessary."

88. See fn. 15.

89. *Weekly Compilation of Presidential Documents*, April 25, 1994, p. 838.

90. *Congressional Record*, July 20, 1994, pp. S 9291-94.

91. Larry Margasak, "87 GOP House members urge Elders' resignation," *Boston Globe*. June 21, 1994.

92. "We've Heard That...," *Washington Post*, June 23, 1994.

93. Daniel Wattenberg, "The Lady Macbeth of Little Rock," *The American Spectator*, August 1992. Wattenberg summarized the revolutionary recommendations given in Mrs. Clinton's 1974 essay, "Children Under the Law," published in 1982 by the *Harvard Educational Review*: "(1) the immediate abolition of the legal status of minority and the reversal of the legal presumption of the incompetence of minors in favor of a presumption of competence; (2) the extension to children of all procedural rights guaranteed to children; (3) the rejection of the legal presumption of the identity of interests between parents and their children, and permission for competent children to assert those independent interests in the courts."

94. Ibid.

95. Ibid.

96. House Committee on Un-American Activities Report # 3123, September 21, 1950.

97. "Selling Health Security," *The New American*, October 18, 1993.

98. Conservative Index, *The New American*, November 2, 1992.

99. Albert Gore, Jr., *Earth in the Balance* (New York: Houghton Miflin, 1992).

100. Dixy Lee Ray, *Environmental Overkill* (Washington, DC: Gateway Regnery, 1993).

101. Anthony Lukas, "The Council On Foreign Relations: Is It a Club? Seminar? Presidium? Invisible

106

Government?" *New York Times Magazine*, November 21, 1971.

102. "Ginsburg Handed Down Sweeping Pro-Quota Decision in 1981: Reversed By Supreme Court," *Human Events*, July 3, 1993.

103. Carol Innerst, "Home-school advocates rip Breyer," *Washington Times*, July 14, 1994.

104. According to the CFR's *Annual Report 1994*, CFR members serving in the U.S. Senate in 1995 include Chafee (R-RI), Cohen (D-ME), Dodd (D-CT), Graham (D-FL), Kerry (D-MA), Lieberman (D-CT), Moynihan (D-NY), Pell (D-RI), Pressler (R-SD), Robb (D-VA), Rockefeller (D-WV), Roth (R-DE), and Snowe (R-ME).

CFR members serving in the House include Berman (D-CA), Gejdenson (D-CT), Gephardt (D-MO), Gingrich (R-GA), Houghton (R-NY), Leach (R-IA), Matsui (D-CA), Petri (R-WI), Richardson (D-NM), Schroeder (D-CO), Spratt (D-SC), Stokes (D-OH), and Torricelli (D-NJ).

The March 23, 1994 membership list published by The Trilateral Commission notes that TC members serving in the U.S. Senate in 1995 include Chafee (R-RI), Cohen (R-ME), Feinstein (D-CA), Robb (D-VA), Rockefeller (D-WV), and Roth (R-DE).

TC members serving in the House include Hamilton (D-IN), Leach (R-IA), and Rangel (D-NY).

105. *The Federalist Papers*, Essay #47.

106. The Tenth Amendment states: "The powers not delegated to the United States by the Constitution, nor prohibited by it to the States, are reserved to the States respectively, or to the people."

107. Richard Harwood, "Ruling Class Journalists," *Washington Post*, October 30, 1993, page A21.

108. The American people are choosing what the John Birch Society has always called for in its motto: "Less government, more responsibility, and — with God's help — a better world."

APPENDICES

Appendix A

COUNCIL ON FOREIGN RELATIONS
Membership Roster, June 1994

Officers

Peter G. Peterson
Chairman of the Board

Jeane J. Kirkpatrick
Vice Chairman of the Board

Leslie H. Gelb
President

Alton Frye
Kenneth H. Keller
Larry L. Fabian
Senior Vice Presidents

Directors

Peter G. Peterson
Paul A. Volcker
James E. Burke
Richard B. Cheney
Robert F. Erburu
Karen Elliott House
William S. Cohen
Joshua Lederberg
Thomas R. Donahue
Robert D. Hormats
John E. Bryson
Maurice R. Greenberg
James R. Houghton

Charlayne Hunter-Gault
Kenneth W. Dam
Rita E. Hauser
E. Gerald Corrigan
Leslie H. Gelb
Paul A. Allaire
Robert E. Allen
Theodore C. Sorensen
Garrick Utley
Carla A. Hills
Helene L. Kaplan
Frank G. Zarb
Robert B. Zoellick

Corporate Member Roster

AGIP Petroleum Company
AGIP, USA
Alliance Capital Management
Amerada Hess Corporation
American Airlines

American Council on Germany
American Express Company
American International Group
American International Petroleum
Archer Daniels Midland

Arnhold and S. Bleichroeder
Arthur Andersen & Company
ASARCO
AT&T International
Atlantic Richfield Company
Avon Products
Backer Spielvogel Bates Worldwide
Baker & McKenzie
Banco Santander
Bank Audi
Bank of America
Bank of Montreal
The Bank of New York
Bankers Trust Company
Banque Paribas
BDO Seidman
BEA Associates
Bear, Stearns & Co.
Becton Dickinson and Company
Bertelsmann Corporation
The Blackstone Group
Bloomberg Financial Markets
BMW of North America
Boeing Corporation
Booz, Allen & Hamilton
Bristol-Myers Squibb Company
British Airways
British-American Chamber of Commerce
Brown Brothers Harriman
Cahill Gordon & Reindell
Caltex Petroleum Corporation
Canadian Imperial Bank of Commerce
Capital Cities/ABC
CDC North America
Champion International Corporation
Chancellor Capital Management
The Chase Manhattan Bank
Chemical Banking Corporation
Chevron
Citibank/Citicorp
Clayton Dubilier & Rice
Cleary, Gottlieb, Steen & Hamilton
The Coca-Cola Company
Coopers & Lybrand
Corning
Coudert Brothers
Davis Polk & Wardwell
Debevoise & Plimpton
Deere & Company
Deutsche Bank AG
Dillon, Read & Company
Dime Savings Bank
Dow Chemical
Dow Jones & Co.
Ernst & Young
Estee Lauder
Executone Information Systems
Exxon Corporation
Fairbanks Management Corporation
The First Boston Corporation
The First National Bank of Chicago

Fischer Francis Trees & Watts
Forbes Magazine
Ford Motor Company
French-American Chamber of Commerce
Gavin Anderson & Company
General Electric Company
Goldman, Sachs & Co.
Guardsmark
H. J. Heinz Company
Hypo-Bank AG
IBJ Schroder Bank & Trust
Institute of International Bankers
International Paper
ITT Corporation
JETRO New York
John A. Levin & Company
Johnson & Johnson
Jones, Day, Reavis & Pogue
J. P. Morgan & Company
Kelly, Drye & Warren
Kohlberg Kravis Roberts & Co.
KPMG Peat Marwick & Company
Lazard Freres & Co.
Lehman Brothers
Loral Corporation
MacAndrews & Forbes
Marks & Murase
Marsh & McLennan
Martin Marietta Corporation
Marubeni America Corporation
Matra Hachette
McKinsey & Company
Mercedes-Benz of North America
Merrill Lynch & Company Foundation
Mine Safety Appliances Company
Mitsui & Co. (U.S.A.)
Mobil Corporation
Morgan Stanley & Co.
National Westminster Bank Plc
Newsweek
The New York Times Company Foundation
Nippon Steel U.S.A.
Nomura Research Institute
NYNEX Corporation
Occidental Petroleum
Olin Corporation
Oxford Analytica
Paul Ray Berndtson
PepsiCo
Pfizer
Poten & Partners
Price Waterhouse & Co.
Procter & Gamble
The Prudential Insurance Company
   of America
The Putnam Companies
Reuters America
The Rockefeller Group
Rogers & Wells
Royal Bank of Canada
Russell Reynolds Associates

RWS Energy Services	Times Mirror
Salomon Brothers	Time Warner
Schlumberger Limited	Titan Industrial Corporation
Scudder, Stevens & Clark Ltd.	Towers Perrin
Shearman & Sterling	Toyota Motor Corporation of North America
Shell Oil Company	The Travelers
Siemens Corporation	TRW
Sierra Capital Management	Tudor Investment Corporation
Simpson, Thacher & Bartlett	Union Camp Corporation
Skandinaviska Enskilda Banken	United Technologies
SmithKline Beecham	U.S. Trust Company of New York
Sony Corporation of America	Viatel
Southern California Edison Company	E. M. Warburg, Pincus & Co.
Spencer Stuart & Associates	S. G. Warburg & Co.
Standard & Poor's Ratings Group	Weil, Gotshal & Manges
Sullivan & Cromwell	White & Case
Summit International Associates	World Gold Council
Texaco	Xerox Corporation
TIAA-CREF	Young & Rubicam

Member Roster

A

Aaron, David L.	Alford, William P.	Apodaca, Jerry
Abboud, A. Robert	Allaire, Paul A.	Appiah, Kwame Anthony
Abboud, Labeeb M.	Allan, F. Aley	Apter, David E.
Abdel-Meguid, Tarek	Allbritton, Joe L.	Araskog, Rand V.
Abegglen, James C.	Allen, Lew, Jr.	Arciniega, Tomas A.
Abel, Elie	Allen, Robert E.	Arcos, Cresencio S.
Abram, Morris B.	Allison, Graham T., Jr.	Arledge, Roone
Abramowitz, Morton I.	Allison, Richard C.	Armacost, Michael H.
Abrams, Elliott	Alpern, Alan N.	Armstrong, Anne
Abshire, David M.	Altman, Roger C.	Armstrong, C. Michael
Aburdene, Odeh	Altman, Sidney	Armstrong, John A.
Ackerman, Peter	Altschul, Arthur G.	Arnhold, Henry H.
Adams, Gordon M.	Alvarado, Donna M.	Arnold, Millard W.
Adams, Robert McCormick	Alvarez, Jose E.	Aron, Adam M.
Adelman, Carol C.	Ames, Oakes	Aronson, Bernard W.
Adelman, Kenneth L.	Amos, Deborah	Aronson, Jonathan D.
Agnew, Harold M.	Andelman, David	Art, Robert J.
Agostinelli, Robert F.	Andersen, Harold W.	Arthurs, Alberta
Agronsky, Martin	Anderson, Craig B.	Artzt, Edwin L.
Aguirre, Horacio	Anderson, David	Asencio, Diego C.
Aho, C. Michael	Anderson, John B.	Asher, Robert E.
Aidinoff, M. Bernard	Anderson, Lisa	Asmus, Ronald D.
Ajami, Fouad	Anderson, Marcus A.	Aspin, Les
Akins, James E.	Anderson, Paul F.	Assevero, Vicki-Ann E.
Albright, Alice Patterson	Anderson, Robert	Assousa, George E.
Albright, Archie E.	Anderson, Robert O.	Atherton, Alfred L., Jr.
Albright, Madeleine	Andreas, Dwayne O.	Atwood, J. Brian
Alderman, Michael H.	Andrews, David R.	Augustine, Norman R.
Aldrich, George H.	Ansour, M. Michael	Auspitz, Josiah Lee
Alexander, Robert J.	Anthoine, Robert	Ausubel, Jesse Huntley
Alexander, Sarah Elizabeth	Anthony, John Duke	Avedon, John F.
	Apgar, David P.	Avery, John E.

B

Babbitt, Bruce
Bacot, J. Carter
Bader, William B.
Baer, M. Delal
Baeza, Mario L.
Bailey, Charles W.
Bains, Leslie E.
Baird, Charles F.
Baker, Howard H., Jr.
Baker, James E.
Baker, Pauline H.
Baker, Stewart A.
Balaran, Paul
Baldwin, David A.
Baldwin, H. Furlong
Baldwin, Richard Edward
Baldwin, Robert E.
Bales, Carter F.
Balick, Kenneth D.
Baliles, Gerald L.
Ball, David G.
Barber, Charles F.
Barber, James A., Jr.
Bardel, William G.
Barger, Teresa C.
Barker, John P.
Barker, Robert R.
Barnds, William J.
Barnes, Harry G., Jr.
Barnes, Michael D.
Barnet, Richard J.
Barnett, A. Doak
Barnett, Michael N.
Barnett, Robert W.
Baroody, William J., Jr.
Barr, Thomas D.
Barrett, Barbara McConnell
Barrett, John A.
Barrett, Nancy Smith
Barry, John
Barry, Lisa B.
Barry, Thomas C.
Bartholomew, Reginald
Bartlett, Joseph W.
Bartlett, Thomas A.
Bartley, Robert L.
Barton, Christopher
Basek, John T.
Bashawaty, Albert C.
Basora, Adrian A.
Bass, James E.
Bass, Peter Evan
Bassow, Whitman
Batkin, Alan R.
Bator, Francis M.
Battle, Lucius D.
Bauman, Robert P.
Baumann, Carol Edler
Baumann, Roger R.
Bean, Atherton

Beard, Ronald S.
Beattie, Richard I.
Becherer, Hans W.
Beckler, David Z.
Beeman, Richard E.
Begley, Louis
Behrman, Jack N.
Beim, David O.
Beinecke, William S.
Belfer, Robert A.
Bell, David E.
Bell, Holley Mack
Bell, J. Bowyer
Bell, Peter D.
Bell, Steve
Bellamy, Carol
Bellinger, John B.
Bello, Judith Hippler
Bell-Rose, Stephanie
Benbow, Terence H.
Bender, Gerald J.
Bennet, Douglas J., Jr.
Bennett, Andrew
Bennett, Donald V.
Bennett, J. F.
Bennett, Susan J.
Bennett, W. Tapley, Jr.
Benson, Lucy Wilson
Beplat, Tristan E.
Berger, Marilyn
Berger, Samuel R.
Berger, Suzanne
Bergold, Harry E., Jr.
Bergsten, C. Fred
Berkowitz, Bruce D.
Berman, Howard L.
Bernardin, Joseph Cardinal
Berndt, John E.
Bernstein, David S.
Bernstein, Peter W.
Bernstein, Robert L.
Berresford, Susan Vail
Berris, Jan
Bessie, Simon Michael
Best, William A., III
Bestor, Theodore
Bestani, Robert M.
Betts, Richard K.
Beyer, John C.
Bialer, Seweryn
Bialkin, Kenneth J.
Bicksler, Barbara
Biel, Eric R.
Biemann, Betsy
Bienen, Henry S.
Bierley, John C.
Biggs, David
Bilder, Richard
Binger, James H.
Binkley, Nicholas B.
Binnendijk, Hans

Birkelund, John P.
Birnbaum, Eugene A.
Bissell, Richard E.
Bjornlund, Eric C.
Black, Joseph E.
Black, Shirley Temple
Black, Stanley Warren
Blacker, Coit Dennis
Blackwell, J. Kenneth
Blackwell, James A., Jr.
Blackwill, Robert D.
Blair, Sally Onesti
Blake, Robert O.
Blake, Vaughn R.
Blank, Stephen
Blechman, Barry M.
Bleier, Edward
Blendon, Robert J.
Blinken, Antony J.
Bliss, Richard M.
Bloch, Julia Chang
Bloom, Evan Todd
Bloomfield, Lincoln P.
Bloomfield, Richard J.
Blum, John A.
Blumenthal, Sidney
Blumenthal, W. Michael
Bob, Daniel E.
Bobbitt, Philip
Bodie, William C.
Boeker, Paul H.
Bogert, Carroll
Boggs, Michael D.
Bohen, Frederick M.
Bohlen, Avis T.
Bohn, John A.
Bolling, Landrum R.
Bollinger, Martin J.
Bond, George C.
Bond, Robert D.
Bonime-Blanc, Andrea
Bonney, J. Dennis
Bonsal, Dudley B.
Bonsal, Philip W.
Booker, Salih
Bookout, John F.
Boone, Theodore S.
Boren, David Lyle
Boschwitz, Rudy
Bossert, Philip A., Jr.
Bosworth, Stephen W.
Botts, John C.
Bouis, Antonina W.
Bouton, Marshall M.
Bovin, Denis A.
Bowen, William G.
Bower, Joseph L.
Bowie, Robert R.
Bowlin, Mike R.
Bowman, Richard C.
Boyd, Charles G.

Boyer, Ernest L.
Bracken, Paul
Brademas, John
Bradford, Zeb
Bradley, Edward R.
Bradley, William L.
Brady, Linda Parrish
Brady, Nicholas F.
Brainard, Lawrence J.
Brainard, S. Lael
Brand, Laurie A.
Branscomb, Lewis M.
Branson, William H.
Brauchli, Marcus W.
Breck, Henry R.
Breindel, Eric M.
Bremer, L. Paul, III
Breslauer, George W.
Bresnan, John J.
Brewer, John Dorsett
Breyer, Stephen G.
Briggs, Everett Ellis
Brimmer, Andrew F.
Brimmer, Esther Diane
Brinkley, David
Brittenham, Raymond L.
Brock, Mitchell
Broda, Frederick C.
Brokaw, Tom
Bromley, D. Allan
Bronfman, Edgar M.
Brookins, Carol
Brooks, Harvey
Brower, Charles N.
Brown, Alice L.
Brown, Carroll
Brown, Frederic J.
Brown, Gwendolyn
Brown, Harold
Brown, L. Carl
Brown, L. Dean
Brown, Lester R.
Brown, Richard P., Jr.
Brown, Ronald H.
Brown, Walter H.
Browne, Robert S.
Bruce, Judith
Bruemmer, Melissa L.S.
Bruemmer, Russell J.
Bryan, Greyson, L.
Bryant, Ralph C.
Bryson, John E.
Brzezinski, Zbigniew
Buchheim, Robert W.
Buchman, Mark E.
Buckley, William F., Jr.
Buergenthal, Thomas
Bugliarello, George
Bullard, Edward P.
Bullock, Mary Brown
Bundy, McGeorge

Bundy, William P.
Burand, Deborah K.
Burgess, John A.
Burke, James E.
Burkhalter, Holly J.
Burley, Anne-Marie
   Slaughter
Burlingame, Edward L.
Burns, Haywood
Burns, Patrick Owen
Burns, William F.
Burns, William J.
Burt, Richard R.
Burton, Daniel F., Jr.
Bushner, Rolland
Bussey, Donald S.
Bussey, John
Busuttil, James
Butler, George Lee
Butler, Samuel C.
Butler, William J.
Byrnes, Robert F.

C

Cabot, Louis W.
Cabot, Thomas D.
Cabranes, Jose A.
Cahill, Kevin M.
Cahn, Anne H.
Cahouet, Frank V.
Calabia, Dawn T.
Calder, Kent Eyring
Caldwell, Dan
Caldwell, Philip
Calhoun, Michael J.
Califano, Joseph A., Jr.
Callander, Robert J.
Callen, Michael A.
Calleo, David P.
Callwood, Kevin R.
Campbell, Colin G.
Campbell, John C.
Campbell, Kurt M.
Campbell, W. Glenn
Camps, Miriam
Canavan, Christopher
Canfield, Franklin O.
Cannon, James M.
Cappello, Juan C.
Carbonell, Nestor T.
Carey, Hugh L.
Carey, John
Carey, Sarah C.
Carey, William D.
Carlos, Manuel Luis
Carlson, Robert J.
Carlson, Steven E.
Carlucci, Frank C., III
Carmichael, William D.
Carnesale, Albert
Carothers, Thomas

Carpendale, Andrew Michael
Carrington, Walter C.
Carrion, Richard L.
Carroll, J. Speed
Carruth, Reba Anne
Carson, C. W., Jr.
Carson, Edward M.
Carswell, Robert
Carter, Ashton B.
Carter, Barry E.
Carter, George E.
Carter, Hodding, III
Carter, Jimmy
Carter, Marshall N.
Casper, Gerhard
Cates, John M., Jr.
Cattarulla, Elliot R.
Catto, Henry E., Jr.
Caulfield, Matthew P.
Cave, Ray
Cebrowski, Arthur K.
Celeste, Richard F.
Cerjan, Paul G.
Chace, James
Chafee, John H.
Chain, John T., Jr.
Challenor, Herschelle S.
Chambers, Anne Cox
Chan, Ronnie C.
Chancellor, John
Chanis, Jonathan A.
Chao, Elaine L.
Chapman, Margaret Holt
Charles, Robert B.
Charney, Jonathan I.
Charpie, Robert A.
Chasin, Dana
Chaudhry, Kiren Aziz
Chavez, Linda
Chayes, Abram J.
Chayes, Antonia Handler
Cheever, Daniel S.
Chen, Kimball C.
Chenault, Kenneth I.
Cheney, Richard B.
Cheremeteff, Kyra
Cherne, Leo
Chickering, A. Lawrence
Choharis, Peter C.
Cholmondeley, Paula H. J.
Choucri, Nazli
Chow, Jack C.
Christianson, Geryld B.
Christman, Daniel William
Christman, Walter L.
Christopher, Warren
Chubb, Hendon
Churchill, Buntzie Ellis
Cisler, Walker L.
Cisneros, Henry G.
Clapp, Priscilla A.

Clark, Dick	Coombe, George W., Jr.	Davidson, Daniel I.
Clark, Howard L., Sr.	Coombs, Philip H.	Davidson, Ralph K.
Clark, J. H. Cullum	Coon, Jane Abell	Davidson, Ralph P.
Clark, Kenneth B.	Cooney, Joan Ganz	Davis, Allison S.
Clark, Noreen	Cooper, Charles A.	Davis, Jacquelyn K.
Clark, Susan Lesley	Cooper, Chester L.	Davis, Jerome
Clark, Wesley K.	Cooper, John Milton	Davis, Kathryn W.
Clarke, J.G.	Cooper, Kerry	Davis, Lynn E.
Clarkson, Lawrence W.	Cooper, Richard N.	Davis, Maceo N.
Clendenin, John L.	Cornelius, Wayne	Davis, Nathaniel
Cleveland, Harlan	Corrigan, E. Gerald	Davis, Vincent
Cleveland, Peter	Corrigan, Kevin	Davison, Daniel P.
Clifford, Donald K., Jr.	Cott, Suzanne	Davison, W. Phillips
Cline, Ray S.	Cotter, William	Dawisha, Karen Lea
Cline, William R.	Courtney, William H.	Dawkins, Peter M.
Clinton, Bill	Cowal, Sally Grooms	Dawson, Christine L.
Cloherty, Patricia M.	Cowan, L. Gray	Dawson, Horace G., Jr.
Cloud, Stanley Wills	Cowhey, Peter F.	Dawson, Horace G., III
Clough, Michael	Cox, Edward F.	Dawson, Marion M.
Clurman, Richard M.	Cox, Robert G.	Day, Anthony
Cobb, Charles E., Jr.	Crahan, Margaret E.	Day, Arthur R.
Cobb, Paul Whitlock, Jr.	Crawford, John F.	Day, Robert A.
Cochran, Barbara S.	Crile, George, III	Deagle, Edwin A., Jr.
Coffey, C. Shelby, III	Crittenden, Ann	Dean, Jonathan
Coffey, Joseph I.	Crocker, Chester A.	Dean, Robert W.
Cohen, Benjamin J.	Cromwell, Adelaide	Debevoise, Eli Whitney, II
Cohen, Eliot A.	Cross, June V.	de Borchgrave, Arnaud
Cohen, Herman J.	Cross, Sam Y.	Debs, Barbara Knowles
Cohen, Jerome Alan	Cross, Theodore	Debs, Richard A.
Cohen, Joel E.	Crossette, Barbara	DeBusk, F. Amanda
Cohen, Patricia	Crowe, William J.	DeCrane, Alfred C., Jr.
Cohen, Roberta	Crystal, Lester M.	Decter, Midge
Cohen, Stephen B.	Cullum, Lee	de Cubas, Jose
Cohen, Stephen F.	Culver, John C.	Dedrick, Fred T.
Cohen, Stephen S.	Cummings, Robert L., Jr.	Deffenbaugh, Ralston H., Jr.
Cohen, William S.	Cummiskey, Frank J.	Deibel, Terry L.
Colbert, Evelyn	Cuneo, Donald	de Janosi, Peter E.
Colby, Jonathan E.	Cuny, Frederic C.	de la Garza, Rodolfo O.
Colby, William E.	Cuomo, Kerry Kennedy	Delaney, Andrew J.
Cole, Johnnetta	Cuomo, Mario M.	del Olmo, Frank
Coleman, Isobel	Curran, R. T.	de Menil, George
Coleman, William T., Jr.	Curtis, Gerald L.	de Menil, Lois Pattison
Collier, David	Cutler, Lloyd N.	Deming, Rust M.
Collins, Joseph J.	Cutler, Walter L.	Denison, Robert J.
Collins, Paula J.	Cutter, W. Bowman	Dennis, Everette E.
Combs, Richard E., Jr.	Cyr, Arthur	Denny, Brewster C.
Comstock, Philip E., Jr.		Denoon, David B. H.
Condon, Joseph F.	**D**	Denton, E. Hazel
Cone, Sydney M., III	Dahlman, Michael K.	DePalma, Samuel
Connolly, Gerald E.	Dale, William B.	Dergham, Raghida
Connor, John T., Jr.	Dalley, George A.	Derian, Patricia Murphy
Considine, Jill M.	Dallin, Alexander	Derryck, Vivian Lowery
Constable, Pamela	Dallmeyer, Dorinda	Desai, Padma
Conway, Jill	Dalton, James E.	Destler, I. M.
Cook, Don	Dam, Kenneth W.	Deutch, John M.
Cook, Frances D.	Damrosch, Lori Fisler	Deutch, Michael J.
Cook, Gary M.	Danforth, William H.	DeVecchi, Robert P.
Cook, Howard A.	Daniel, Ana R.	Devine, Thomas J.
Cooke, Goodwin	Daniel, D. Ronald	de Vries, Rimmer
Cooke, John F.	Danner, Mark	DeWind, Adrian W.
Coolidge, Nicholas J.	David, Jack	DeYoung, Karen

116

Dickey, Christopher S.	**E**	Falk, Richard A.
Dickson, R. Russell, Jr.	Eagleburger, Lawrence S.	Fallows, James
Didion, Joan	Earle, Ralph, II	Fanning, Katherine W.
Diebold, John	East, Maurice A.	Fanton, Jonathan F.
Diebold, William, Jr.	Easum, Donald B.	Farer, Tom J.
Diehl, Jackson	Eberle, William D.	Farmer, Thomas L.
Dilenschneider, Robert L.	Eccles, Peter W.	Fascell, Dante B.
Dillon, Douglas	Ecton, Donna R.	Fawaz, Leila
Di Martino, Rita	Edelman, Albert I.	Feaver, Peter D.
Dine, Thomas A.	Edelman, Gerald M.	Feierstein, Mark
Djerejian, Edward P.	Edelman, Marian Wright	Feiner, Ava S.
Dobriansky, Paula	Edelstein, Julius C.C.	Feinstein, Lee
Dodd, Christopher J.	Edley, Christopher, Jr.	Feissel, Gustave
Doherty, William C., Jr.	Edwards, Howard L.	Feith, Douglas J.
Dominguez, Jorge I.	Edwards, Robert H., Jr.	Feldman, Mark B.
Donahue, Thomas R.	Ehrlich, Thomas	Feldstein, Martin S.
Donaldson, Robert H.	Eilts, Hermann Frederick	Feltman, Jeffrey
Donaldson, William H.	Einaudi, Luigi R.	Fenster, Steven R.
Donnell, Ellsworth	Einhorn, Jessica P.	Ferguson, Glenn W.
Donnelly, H. C.	Eisendrath, Charles R.	Ferguson, James L.
Donnelly, Sally B.	Eizenstat, Stuart E.	Ferguson, William C.
Doran, Charles F.	Eliason, Leslie C.	Ferrari, Frank E.
Dornbusch, Rudiger	Eliot, Theodore L., Jr.	Ferraro, Geraldine A.
Doty, Paul M., Jr.	Elliott, Inger McCabe	Ferre, Antonio Luis
Dougan, Diana Lady	Elliott, Osborn	Ferre, Maurice A.
Douglass, Robert R.	Ellis, James R.	Fesharaki, Fereidun
Downie, Leonard, Jr.	Ellis, Patricia	Feshbach, Murray
Doyle, James S.	Ellison, Keith P.	Fessenden, Hart
Doyle, Michael William	Ellsberg, Daniel	Fetter, Steve
Draper, William H., III	Ellsworth, Robert F.	Fierce, Milfred C.
Drayton, William, Jr.	Ely, John Hart	Fifield, Russell H.
Drell, Sidney D.	Ely-Raphel, Nancy Halliday	Finberg, Barbara D.
Drew, Elizabeth	Embree, Ainslie T.	Finger, Seymour Maxwell
Dreyfuss, Joel	Emerson, Alice F.	Finkelstein, Lawrence S.
Drobnick, Richard	Enders, Thomas O.	Finlayson, Grant Ellis
Drumwright, J. R.	Enthoven, Alain	Finn, James
Druyan, Ann	Epstein, Jason	Finnemore, Martha
Duberstein, Kenneth M.	Epstein, Joshua M.	Finney, Paul B.
Dubow, Arthur M.	Erb, Guy F.	Firmage, Edwin B.
DuBrul, Stephen M., Jr.	Erb, Richard D.	Fischer, David J.
Duderstadt, James J.	Erbsen, Claude E.	Fischer, Stanley
Duersten, Althea L.	Erburu, Robert F.	Fisher, Cathleen S.
Duffey, Joseph	Ercklentz, Alexander T.	Fisher, Peter Reyerson
Duffy, Gloria Charmian	Estabrook, Robert H.	Fisher, Richard W.
Duffy, James H.	Estrada, Alfredo	Fisher, Roger
Dugan, Michael J.	Esty, Daniel C.	Fishlow, Albert
Dukakis, Michael S.	Evans, Carol V.	FitzGerald, Frances
Duke, Angier Biddle	Evans, Gordon W.	Fitzgibbons, Harold E.
Dulany, Peggy	Evans, Harold M.	Fitz-Pegado, Lauri J.
Duncan, Charles W., Jr.	Evans, John C.	Flaherty, Peter
Duncan, John C.	Evans, Rowland, Jr.	Flanagan, Stephen J.
Duncan, Richard L.	Everingham, Susan M. S.	Flanigan, Peter M.
Dunigan, P. Andrew	Ewing, William, Jr.	Fletcher, Phillip Douglas
Dunkerley, Craig G.		Flournoy, Michele A.
Dunlop, Joan Banks	**F**	Flynn, Stephen E.
Dunn, Kempton		Fogleman, Ronald R.
Dunn, Lewis A.	Fabian, Larry L.	Foley, S. R., Jr.
Dutton, Frederick G.	Fairbanks, Douglas, Jr.	Foley, Thomas S.
Duval, Michael Raoul	Fairbanks, Richard M., III	Foote, Edward T., II
Dyke, Nancy Bearg	Falco, Mathea	Ford, Gerald R.
	Falcoff, Mark	Ford, Paul B., Jr.
	Falk, Pamela S.	

Forester, Lynn
Forman, Shepard
Forrester, Anne
Fort, Randall M.
Fosler, Gail
Foster, Brenda Lei
Foulon, Mark
Fowler, Henry H.
Fox, Donald T.
Fox, Eleanor M.C.
Fox, Joseph C.
Franck, Thomas M.
Francke, Albert, III
Frank, Charles R., Jr.
Frank, Isaiah
Frank, Richard A.
Frankel, Francine R.
Franklin, Barbara Hackman
Franklin, George S.
Fredericks, J. Wayne
Freeman, Bennett
Freeman, Harry L.
Freeman, Orville L.
Freidheim, Cyrus F., Jr.
Frelinghuysen, Peter H.B.
Fremont-Smith, Marion R.
Freund, Gerald
Frey, Donald N.
Freytag, Richard A.
Fribourg, Michel
Fribourg, Paul
Fried, Edward R.
Friedman, Benjamin M.
Friedman, David S.
Friedman, Stephen
Friedman, Stephen J.
Friedman, Thomas L.
Frieman, Wendy
Friend, Theodore
Fromkin, David
Fromm, Joseph
Froot, Kenneth A.
Frost, Ellen L.
Fry, Earl H.
Frye, Alton
Fuerbringer, Otto
Fukushima, Glen S.
Fukuyama, Francis
Fuller, Kathryn S.
Fuller, William P.
Fullerton, William Bewick
Furlaud, Richard M.
Futter, Ellen V.

G

Gabriel, Charles A.
Gaddis, John Lewis
Gaer, Felice
Galbraith, Evan G.
Gallagher, Dennis
Gallucci, Robert L.

Galpin, Timothy J.
Galvin, John R.
Galvis, Sergio J.
Ganguly, Sumit
Gann, Pamela
Ganoe, Charles S.
Garcia-Passalacqua, Juan Manuel
Gard, Robert G., Jr.
Gardels, Nathan P.
Gardner, James A.
Gardner, Nina Luzzato
Gardner, Richard N.
Garment, Leonard
Garment, Suzanne
Garrison, Mark
Gart, Murray J.
Garten, Jeffrey E.
Garthoff, Raymond L.
Garwin, Richard L.
Gates, Henry Louis, Jr.
Gates, Philomene A.
Gates, Robert M.
Gati, Charles
Gati, Toby Trister
Gaudiani, Claire Lynn
Gause, F. Gregory, III
Gay, Catherine
Geertz, Clifford
Geier, Philip O.
Geiger, Theodore
Gejdenson, Sam
Gelb, Leslie H.
Gelb, Richard L.
Gell-Mann, Murray
Gellman, Barton David
Georgescu, Peter A.
Gephardt, Richard A.
Gerber, Louis
Gergen, David R.
Gerhart, Gail M.
Germain, Adrienne
Gerschel, Patrick A.
Gershman, Carl
Gerson, Ralph J.
Gerstner, Louis V., Jr.
Getler, Michael
Geyelin, Henry R.
Geyelin, Philip L.
Geyer, Georgie Anne
Gfoeller, Joachim, Jr.
Ghiglione, Loren
Gibbons, John H.
Gibbs, Nancy Reid
Gibney, Frank B.
Gibney, James Suydam
Giffen, James H.
Gilbert, Jackson B.
Gilbert, Jarobin, Jr.
Gilbert, Steven J.
Gillespie, Michael J.

Gilmore, Kenneth O.
Gilmore, Richard
Gilpatric, Roswell L.
Gilpin, Robert G., Jr.
Gingrich, Newton L.
Ginsburg, David
Ginsburg, Jane
Ginsburg, Ruth Bader
Glauber, Robert R.
Glazer, Nathan
Gleysteen, William H., Jr.
Globerman, Norma
Gluck, Carol
Gluck, Frederick W.
Godchaux, Frank A., III
Godwin, I. Lamond
Goekjian, Samuel V.
Goheen, Robert F.
Goins, Charlynn
Goizueta, Roberto C.
Goldberg, Andrew C.
Goldberg, Samuel
Goldberger, Marvin L.
Golden, James R.
Golden, William T.
Goldin, Harrison J.
Goldman, Andrew
Goldman, Charles N.
Goldman, Emily O.
Goldman, Guido
Goldman, Marshall I.
Goldman, Merle
Goldmark, Peter C., Jr.
Goldring, Natalie J.
Goldschmidt, Neil
Goldsmith, Jack Landman, III
Goldwyn, David L.
Golightly, Niel L.
Golob, Paul D.
Gomory, Ralph E.
Gompert, David C.
Goodby, James E.
Goodman, George J. W.
Goodman, Herbert I.
Goodman, John B.
Goodman, Roy M.
Goodpaster, Andrew J.
Goodsell, James Nelson
Gordon, Albert H.
Gordon, Lincoln
Gordon, Michael R.
Gordon, Philip H.
Gorman, Joseph T.
Gornick, Alan L.
Gotbaum, Victor
Gottemoeller, Rose E.
Gottfried, Kurt
Gottlieb, Gidon A.G.
Gottsegen, Peter M.
Gould, Peter G.

Gourevitch, Peter A.	Haig, Alexander M., Jr.	Heckscher, August
Graff, Henry F.	Hakim, Peter	Hedstrom, Mitchell W.
Graff, Robert D.	Halaby, Najeeb E.	Heep-Richter, Barbara D.
Graham, Bob	Hall, John P.	Heginbotham, Stanley J.
Graham, Katharine	Hallingby, Paul, Jr.	Hehir, J. Bryan
Graham, Thomas, Jr.	Halperin, Morton H.	Heifetz, Elaine F.
Graham, Thomas Wallace	Halsted, Thomas A.	Heilbrunn, Jacob
Grant, James P.	Haltzel, Michael	Heimann, John G.
Grant, Stephen A.	Hamburg, David A.	Heimowitz, James B.
Graubard, Stephen R.	Hamburg, Margaret Ann	Heineman, Benjamin W., Jr.
Graves, Howard D.	Hamilton, Ann O.	Heintzen, Harry L.
Gray, Charles D.	Hamilton, Charles V.	Helander, Robert C.
Gray, Hanna Holborn	Hamilton, Daniel	Heldring, Frederick
Green, Bill	Hamilton, Doug N.	Heller, Richard M.
Green, Carl J.	Hamilton, Edward K.	Hellman, F. Warren
Green, Jerrold D.	Hamilton, Michael P.	Hellmann, Donald C.
Greenberg, Arthur N.	Hamilton, Ruth Simms	Helmboldt, Niles E.
Greenberg, Maurice R.	Hancock, Ellen	Helms, Richard
Greenberg, Sanford D.	Hanrieder, Wolfram F.	Hendrickson, David C.
Greenberger, Robert S.	Hanscom, Patricia L.	Henkin, Alice H.
Greene, James C.	Hansell, Herbert J.	Henkin, Louis
Greene, Joseph N., Jr.	Hansen, Carol Rae	Hennessy, John M.
Greene, Margaret L.	Hansen, Keith Eric	Henninger, Daniel P.
Greene, Wade	Hanson, Thor	Henrikson, Alan K.
Greenfield, James L.	Hantz, Giselle P.	Hentges, Harriet
Greenfield, Meg	Harari, Maurice	Herberger, Roy A., Jr.
Greenspan, Alan	Harding, Harry	Herbst, Jeffrey
Greenwald, Joseph A.	Hardt, John P.	Hermann, Charles F.
Greenway, H. D. S.	Hargrove, John Lawrence	Hernandez, Antonia
Greenwood, Ted	Harleston, Bernard W.	Hernandez-Colon, Rafael
Gregg, Donald P.	Harman, Sidney	Herskovits, Jean
Gregorian, Vartan	Harpel, James W.	Herter, Christian A., Jr.
Grenier, Richard	Harper, Conrad K.	Herter, Frederic P.
Griffith, William E.	Harriman, Pamela C.	Hertzberg, Arthur
Grimes, Joseph A., Jr.	Harris, Irving B.	Hertzberg, Hendrik
Grose, Peter	Harris, John M.	Herz, Barbara
Gross, Patrick W.	Harris, Joseph E.	Herzfeld, Charles M.
Grove, Brandon H., Jr.	Harris, Martha Caldwell	Herzstein, Jessica
Groves, Ray J.	Harrison, Selig S.	Herzstein, Robert E.
Grundfest, Joseph	Harsch, Joseph C.	Hesburgh, Theodore M.
Grune, George V.	Harshberger, Edward R.	Hess, John B.
Grunwald, Henry A.	Hart, Augustin S., Jr.	Hessler, Curtis A.
Guerra-Mondragon, Gabriel	Hart, Parker T.	Hester, James M.
Guest, Michael E.	Hartman, Arthur A.	Hewitt, William A.
Guisinger, Stephen E.	Haskell, John H.F., Jr.	Hewlett, Sylvia Ann
Gullion, Edmund A.	Haskins, Caryl P.	Heyns, Roger W.
Gutfreund, John H.	Hatfield, Robert S.	Hicks, Irvin
Guthman, Edwin O.	Hauge, John R.	Higgins, Robert F.
Gutmann, Henning P.	Hauser, Rita E.	Highet, Keith
Gwertzman, Bernard M.	Hauser, William L.	Hight, B. Boyd
Gwin, Catherine	Hawkins, Ashton	Hill, J. French
	Hawley, F. William	Hill, J. Tomilson
H	Hayek, Alexandre	Hill, Pamela
	Hayes, Margaret Daly	Hillenbrand, Martin J.
Haas, Peter E.	Haynes, Fred	Hillgren, Sonja
Haas, Robert D.	Haynes, Ulric, Jr.	Hills, Carla A.
Haass, Richard N.	Hayward, Thomas B.	Hills, Laura Hume
Haddad, Yvonne Yazbeck	Hazard, John N.	Hilsman, Roger
Hadley, Stephen J.	Healy, Harold H., Jr.	Hilton, Robert P.
Hafner, Joseph A., Jr.	Heard, Alexander	Himes, James A.
Haggard, Stephan	Heck, Charles B.	Hinerfeld, Ruth J.
Hahn, Keith D.		

Hines, Rachel	Huebner, Lee W.	Jacobson, Harold K.
Hinshaw, Randall	Hufbauer, Gary C.	Jacobson, Jerome
Hinton, Deane R.	Huffington, Roy M.	Jacoby, Tamar
Hirschman, Albert O.	Hufstedler, Shirley	Jamieson, J. K.
Hoagland, Jim	Hughes, Jeffrey L.	Janis, Mark W.
Hoar, Joseph P.	Hughes, John	Janklow, Morton L.
Hoch, Frank W.	Hughes, Thomas L.	Janow, Merit E.
Hodgson, James D.	Huizenga, John W.	Jansen, Marius B.
Hoeber, Amoretta M.	Hultman, Tamela	Jaquette, Jane
Hoehn, William E., Jr.	Hume, Ellen	Jarvis, Nancy A.
Hoenlein, Malcolm	Hummel, Arthur W., Jr.	Jastrow, Robert
Hoepli, Nancy L.	Hunsberger, Warren S.	Jeffries, Bradley C.
Hoffman, Adonis Edward	Hunter, Robert E.	Jervis, Robert L.
Hoffman, Michael L.	Hunter, Shireen T.	Jessup, Alpheus W.
Hoffmann, Stanley	Hunter-Gault, Charlayne	Jessup, Philip C., Jr.
Hoge, James F., Jr.	Huntington, Samuel P.	Joffe, Robert D.
Hoge, Warren	Huntsman, Jon M., Jr.	Johns, Lionel Skipwith
Hoguet, George R.	Hurewitz, J. C.	Johnson, Howard W.
Hohenberg, John	Hurford, John B.	Johnson, James A.
Hoinkes, Mary Elizabeth	Hurlock, James B.	Johnson, L. Oakley
Holbrooke, Richard C.	Hurst, Robert J.	Johnson, Larry D.
Holcomb, M. Staser	Hurwitz, Sol	Johnson, Lionel C.
Holl, Jane E.	Huyck, Philip M.	Johnson, Robbin S.
Holland, Mary S.	Hyde, Henry B.	Johnson, Robert W., IV
Hollick, Ann L.	Hyland, William G.	Johnson, Robert H.
Holloway, Dwight F., Jr.	Hyman, Allen I.	Johnson, Suzanne Nora
Holmes, H. Allen		Johnson, Thomas S.
Holt, Pat M.	**I**	Johnson, W. Thomas
Hood, Robert E.		Johnson, Willard R.
Hooks, Benjamin L.	Ignatius, David	Jones, David C.
Hoopes, Townsend W.	Ikenberry, G. John	Jones, James R.
Hope, Judith R.	Ikle, Fred C.	Jones, Sidney R.
Horelick, Arnold L.	Ilchman, Alice S.	Jones, Thomas V.
Horlick, Gary N.	Inderfurth, Karl F.	Jordan, Amos A.
Hormats, Robert D.	Ingersoll, Robert S.	Jordan, Vernon E., Jr.
Horn, Garfield H.	Ink, Dwight	Jorden, William J.
Horn, Karen N.	Inman, B. R.	Joseph, Geri M.
Horn, Miriam	Intriligator, Michael D.	Joseph, James A.
Horn, Sally K.	Irish, Leon E.	Joseph, Richard A.
Horner, Matina S.	Irvin, Patricia L.	Josephson, William
Horowitz, Irving Louis	Irwin, John N., II	Joyce, John T.
Horton, Alan W.	Isaacson, Walter	Junz, Helen B.
Horton, Frank B., III	Iselin, John Jay	Juster, Kenneth I.
Hosmer, Bradley C.	Isenberg, Steven L.	
Hoston, Germaine A.	Isham, Christopher	**K**
Hottelet, Richard C.	Ispahani, Mahnaz Z.	
Houghton, Amory, Jr.	Istel, Yves-Andre	Kahan, Jerome H.
Houghton, James R.	Izlar, William H., Jr.	Kahin, George McT.
House, Karen Elliott		Kahler, Miles
Hovey, Graham	**J**	Kahn, Harry
Hovey, J. Allan, Jr.		Kaiser, Philip M.
Howard, A. E. Dick	Jabber, Paul	Kaiser, Robert G.
Howard, John R.	Jacklin, Nancy P.	Kalb, Bernard
Howell, Ernest M.	Jackson, Bruce P.	Kalb, Marvin
Hoyt, Mont P.	Jackson, Jesse L.	Kalicki, Jan
Huber, Richard L.	Jackson, John H.	Kamarck, Andrew M.
Huber, Robert T.	Jackson, Lois M.	Kamarck, Elaine Ciulla
Huberman, Benjamin	Jackson, Sarah	Kaminer, Peter H.
Hudson, Manley O., Jr.	Jackson, William E.	Kaminsky, Howard
Hudson, Michael C.	Jacob, John E.	Kampelman, Max M.
Hudson, Stewart	Jacobs, Eli S.	Kamsky, Virginia A.
	Jacobs, Nehama	Kanak, Donald Perry
	Jacobs, Norman	

Kandell, Jonathan
Kanet, Roger E.
Kann, Peter R.
Kanter, Arnold
Kanter, Rosabeth Moss
Kaplan, Gilbert E.
Kaplan, Harold J.
Kaplan, Helene L.
Kaplan, Mark N.
Kaplan, Stephen S.
Kapp, Robert A.
Karalekas, Anne
Karamanian, Susan L.
Karis, Thomas G.
Karl, Terry Lynn
Karnow, Stanley
Karns, Margaret P.
Kasdin, Robert
Kass, Stephen L.
Kassof, Allen H.
Katz, Abraham
Katz, Milton
Katz, Ronald S.
Katz, Stanley N.
Katzenbach, Nicholas deB.
Katzenstein, Peter J.
Kaufman, Daniel J.
Kaufman, Henry
Kaufmann, William W.
Kaysen, Carl
Kazemi, Farhad
Kean, Thomas H.
Kearns, David T.
Keel, Alton G., Jr.
Keene, Lonnie S.
Keeny, Spurgeon M., Jr.
Kelleher, Catherine M.
Kellen, Stephen M.
Keller, Edmond J.
Keller, Kenneth H.
Kellerman, Barbara
Kelley, P. X.
Kelly, James P.
Kelly, John H.
Kelman, Herbert C.
Kemble, Eugenia
Kemp, Geoffrey
Kempe, Frederick
Kempner, Maximilian W.
Kendall, Donald M.
Kenen, Peter B.
Keniston, Kenneth
Kennan, Christopher J.
Kennan, Elizabeth T.
Kennan, George F.
Kenney, F. Donald
Kent, William H.
Keohane, Nannerl O.
Keohane, Robert O.
Kerr, Ann Z.
Kerry, John F.

Kessler, Martha Neff
Kester, John G.
Kester, W. Carl
Khalilzad, Zalmay M.
Khuri, Nicola N.
Kiermaier, John
Kiernan, Robert Edward, III
Kiley, Robert R.
Kim, Andrew B.
Kim, Hanya Marie
Kimmitt, Robert M.
King, Henry L.
King, John A., Jr.
King, Kay
Kintner, William R.
Kipper, Judith
Kirk, Grayson L.
Kirkland, Lane
Kirkpatrick, Jeane J.
Kirkpatrick, Melanie
Kissinger, Henry A.
Kitchen, Helen
Kitchen, Jeffrey C.
Kleiman, Robert
Klein, David
Klein, Edward
Klein, Joe
Klissas, Nicholas S.
Klurfeld, James
Knight, Jessie J., Jr.
Knight, Robert Huntington
Knoppers, Antonie T.
Knowlton, William A.
Koch, Wendy M.
Kolodziej, Edward A.
Kolt, George
Koltai, Steven R.
Komisar, Lucy
Kondracke, Morton
Korb, Lawrence J.
Korbonski, Andrzej
Korry, Edward M.
Kotecha, Mahesh K.
Kraar, Louis
Kraemer, Lillian E.
Kramer, Helen M.
Kramer, Jane
Kramer, Mark Nathan
Kramer, Michael
Kramer, Steven Philip
Krasner, Stephen D.
Krasno, Richard M.
Krause, Lawrence B.
Krauss, Clifford
Krauthammer, Charles
Kravis, Henry R.
Kreisberg, Paul H.
Krens, Thomas
Krepinevich, Andrew F.
Krepon, Michael
Kreps, Juanita M.

Krisher, Bernard
Kristoff, Sandra Jeanne
Kristol, Irving
Krueger, Anne O.
Kruidenier, David
Kruzel, Joseph
Ku, Charlotte
Kubarych, Roger M.
Kubisch, Jack B.
Kuchins, Andrew
Kuniholm, Bruce R.
Kunstadter, Geraldine
Kuntz, Carol R.
Kupchan, Charles A.
Kupperman, Robert H.
Kurth, James R.
Kurtzer, Daniel C.
Kyle, Robert D.

L

Laber, Jeri
Labrecque, Thomas G.
Ladner, Joyce A.
Lagon, Mark
Laipson, Ellen
Lake, W. Anthony
Lake, William T.
Lall, Betty Goetz
Lamb, Denis
Lambeth, Benjamin S.
Lamm, Donald S.
Lamont, Lansing
Lampley, Virginia A.
Lampton, David M.
Lancaster, Carol J.
Landau, Christopher
Landau, George W.
Landers, James M.
Landy, Joanne
Lane, Charles M.
Laney, James T.
Langdon, George D., Jr.
Lansner, Kermit I
LaPalombara, Joseph
Lapham, Lewis H.
Lapidus, Gail W.
Larrabee, F. Stephen
Larson, Charles R.
Lary, Hal B.
Lash, Jonathan
Lateef, Noel V.
Lauder, Leonard A.
Laudicina, Paul A.
Lauinger, Philip C., Jr.
Lautenbach, Ned C.
Laventhol, David A.
Lawrence, Richard D.
Lawrence, Robert Z.
Lawson, Eugene K.
Layne, Christopher
Lazarus, Steven

Leach, James	Lincoln, Edward J.	Lynn, James T.
Lederberg, Joshua	Lind, Michael E.	Lynn, Laurence E., Jr.
Lederer, Ivo John	Lindquist, Warren T.	Lyon, David W.
Lee, Ernest S.	Lindsay, Franklin A.	Lyons, Gene M.
Lee, Janet	Lindsay, George N.	Lyons, James E.
Lee, William L.	Lindsay, John V.	Lyons, Richard K.
Lefever, Ernest W.	Lindsay, Robert V.	
Leghorn, Richard S.	Link, Troland S.	**M**
Legvold, Robert H.	Linowes, David F.	Ma, Christopher Yi-Wen
Lehman, John F.	Linowitz, Sol M.	MacArthur, Douglas, II
Lehman, Orin	Lipper, Kenneth	MacCormack, Charles F.
Lehman, Ronald F., II	Lippman, Thomas W.	MacDonald, Gordon J.
Lehrer, Jim	Lipscomb, Thomas H.	MacFarquhar, Emily
Leich, John Foster	Lipset, Seymour Martin	MacGregor, Ian K.
Leigh, Monroe	Lipsky, Seth	Mack, Kathryn S.
Leland, Marc E.	Lipson, Leon	Mackay, Leo S., Jr.
Lelyveld, Joseph	Lissakers, Karin M.	MacLaury, Bruce K.
LeMelle, Tilden J.	Little, David	Macomber, John D.
LeMelle, Wilbert J.	Livingston, Robert Gerald	Macomber, William B.
Lempert, Robert J.	Llewellyn, J. Bruce	Macy, Robert M., Jr.
Lenzen, Louis C.	Lodal, Jan M.	Madrid, Arturo
LeoGrande, William M.	Lodge, George C.	Magowan, Peter A.
Leonard, James F.	Loeb, Frances Lehman	Maguire, John D.
Leonard, James G.	Loeb, John L.	Mahaney, Mark
Leone, Richard C.	Loeb, Marshall	Mahnken, Thomas G.
Lescaze, Lee	Logan, Francis D.	Mahoney, Catherine F.
Lesch, Ann Mosely	Long, T. Dixon	Mahoney, Margaret E.
Lesser, Ian O.	Longstreth, Bevis	Mahoney, Thomas H., IV
Levin, Gerald M.	Loomis, Henry	Mai, Vincent A.
Levin, Michael S.	Loranger, Donald E., Jr.	Maier, Charles S.
Levine, Irving R.	Lord, Bette Bao	Makins, Christopher J.
Levine, Mel	Lord, Winston	Mako, William P.
Levine, Susan B.	Lorena, Inmaculada de	Malek, Frederic V.
Levitas, Mitchel	Habsburgo	Malin, Clement B.
Levy, Marion J., Jr.	Louis, William Roger	Mallery, Richard
Levy, Reynold	Louw, Sharon Freeman	Malmgren, Harald B.
Levy, Walter J.	Lovejoy, Thomas E.	Malmgren, Karen Philippa
Lewis, Anthony	Lovelace, Jon B.	Manca, Marie Antoinette
Lewis, Bernard	Low, Stephen	Mandelbaum, Michael E.
Lewis, Edward T.	Lowenfeld, Andreas F.	Manilow, Lewis
Lewis, Flora	Lowenstein, James G.	Mann, Michael D.
Lewis, John P.	Lowenthal, Abraham F.	Mann, Thomas E.
Lewis, John Wilson	Loy, Frank E.	Manning, Bayless
Lewis, Samuel W.	Lozano, Ignacio E., Jr.	Marans, J. Eugene
Lewis, W. Stephen R.	Lubin, Nancy	Marcum, John Arthur
Lewis, W. Walker	Lubman, Stanley B.	Marder, Murrey
Lewy, Glen S.	Lucas, C. Payne	Marer, Paul
Li, Lehmann	Luce, Charles F.	Margolis, David I.
Li, Victor H.	Luck, Edward C.	Mark, David E.
Libby, I. Lewis	Lucy, William	Mark, Gregory A.
Lichtblau, John H.	Luers, Wendy W.	Mark, Hans M.
Lichtenstein, Cynthia C.	Luers, William H.	Marks, Leonard H.
Lieber, Robert J.	Luke, John A., Jr.	Marks, Paul A.
Lieberman, Henry R.	Lumpe, Lora	Marks, Russell E., Jr.
Lieberman, Joseph I.	Lustick, Ian S.	Marlin, Alice Tepper
Lieberman, Nancy A.	Luttwak, Edward N.	Marmor, Theodore R.
Lieberthal, Kenneth	Lyall, Katharine C.	Marr, Phebe A.
Lief, Louise	Lyman, Princeton Nathan	Marron, Donald B.
Lifton, Robert K.	Lyman, Richard W.	Marshall, Andrew W.
Light, Timothy	Lynch, Edward S.	Marshall, Anthony D.
Lilienthal, Sally	Lynk, Myles V.	Marshall, C. Burton

Marshall, Dale Rogers
Marshall, Katherine
Marshall, Ray
Martin, Daniel R.
Martin, Edwin M.
Martin, Lynn
Martin, Malcolm W.
Martin, Susan Forbes
Martin, William F.
Martin, William McC., Jr.
Martin-Brown, Joan
Martinez, Vilma S.
Martinuzzi, Leo S., Jr.
Marton, Kati
Marx, Anthony
Masin, Michael T.
Mason, Elvis L.
Massie, Suzanne
Mathews, Jessica Tuchman
Mathews, Michael S.
Mathias, Charles McC., Jr.
Mathis, Brian Pierre
Matlock, Jack F.
Matsui, Robert T.
Matteson, William B.
Mattox, Gale A.
Maxwell, Kenneth
May, Ernest R.
Mayer, Claudette
Mayer, Gerald M., Jr.
Mayer, Lawrence A.
Mayhew, Alice E.
Maynes, Charles William
Mazarr, Michael J.
Mazur, Jay
McAfee, W. Gage
McAllister, Jef Olivarius
McCaffrey, Barry R.
McCall, H. Carl
McCann, Edward
McCarthy, James P.
McCarthy, John G.
McCauley, John F.
McCloy, John J., II
McColough, C. Peter
McCormack, Elizabeth J.
McCouch, Donald G.
McCracken, Paul W.
McCurdy, Dave K.
McDonald, Alonzo L.
McDonough, William J.
McDougal, Myres S.
McDougall, Gay J.
McFarlane, Robert C.
McFate, Patricia Ann
McGhee, George C.
McGiffert, David E.
McGillicuddy, John F.
McGovern, George S.
McGowan, Alan
McGrath, Eugene R.

McGuire, Raymond J.
McHale, Thomas R.
McHenry, Donald F.
McKinney, Robert
McLaughlin, David T.
McLean, Sheila Avrin
McLin, Jon B.
McManus, Jason D.
McNamara, Robert S.
McNeill, John H.
McNeill, Robert L.
McPeak, Merrill A.
McPherson, M. Peter
McQuade, Lawrence C.
McWade, Robert
Mead, Dana G.
Meagher, Robert F.
Mearsheimer, John J.
Medish, Mark
Meers, Sharon I.
Mehta, Ved
Meissner, Charles F.
Meissner, Doris M.
Meister, Irene W.
Mello, Judy Hendren
Melloan, George R.
Melville, Richard A.
Mendlovitz, Saul H.
Menke, John R.
Merkling, Christian
Meron, Theodor
Merow, John E.
Merrill, Philip
Merritt, Jack N.
Merszei, Zoltan
Mesa-Lago, Carmelo
Meselson, Matthew
Messner, William Curtis, Jr.
Metcalf, George R.
Mettler, Ruben F.
Meyer, Cord
Meyer, Edward C.
Meyer, John R.
Meyer, Karl E.
Meyerman, Harold J.
Meyerson, Martin
Michaels, Marguerite
Mickelson, Sig
Mickiewicz, Ellen P.
Midgley, Elizabeth
Mihaly, Eugene B.
Mikell, Gwendolyn
Miles, Edward L.
Miller, Charles D.
Miller, Christopher D.
Miller, David Charles, Jr.
Miller, Franklin C.
Miller, J. Irwin
Miller, Judith
Miller, Linda B.
Miller, Marcia E.

Miller, Matthew L.
Miller, Michelle Beth
Miller, Paul David
Miller, Robert Stevens, Jr.
Miller, Roberta Balstad
Miller, William Green
Millett, Allan R.
Millington, John A.
Mills, Bradford
Mills, Susan
Min, Nancy-Ann
Minow, Newton N.
Miranda, Lourdes, R.
Mitchell, George H., Jr.
Mitchell, George J.
Mitchell, Jacquelyn A.
Mitchell, Wandra
Mochizuki, Kiichi
Mochizuki, Mike Masato
Moe, Sherwood G.
Mondale, Walter F.
Monroe, Hunter
Montgomery, George Cranwell
Montgomery, Parker G.
Montgomery, Philip O'Bryan, III
Moock, Joyce Lewinger
Moody, Jim
Moody, William S.
Moore, John M.
Moore, John Norton
Moore, Jonathan
Moore, Julia A.
Moore, Paul, Jr.
Moorman, Thomas S., Jr.
Moose, George E.
Moose, Richard M.
Moran, Theodore H.
Morgan, Thomas E.
Morgenthau, Lucinda L. Franks
Morley, James William
Morrell, Gene P.
Morris, Bailey
Morris, Max K.
Morris, Milton D.
Morrisett, Lloyd N.
Morse, Edward L.
Morse, F. Bradford
Morse, Kenneth P.
Mortimer, David
Moses, Alfred H.
Mosettig, Michael
Moskow, Kenneth A.
Moss, Ambler H., Jr.
Motley, Joel W.
Mottahedeh, Roy
Motulsky, Dan T.
Moynihan, Daniel P.
Mroz, John Edwin

Mudd, Margaret F.	Nix, Crystal	Owen, Henry
Mujal-Leon, Eusebio	Nolan, Janne E.	Owen, Roberts B.
Mulford, David C.	Noland, Marcus	Owens, James W.
Mulholland, William D.	Nolte, Richard H.	Owens, William A.
Muller, Henry	Nooter, Robert H.	Oxman, Stephen A.
Muller, Steven	Norman, William S.	Oxnam, Robert B.
Mundy, Carl E., Jr.	Norton, Augustus Richard	
Munger, Edwin S.	Norton, Eleanor Holmes	**P**
Munroe, George B.	Noto, Lucio A.	Paal, Douglas H.
Munyan, Winthrop R.	Novak, Michael	Pachon, Harry
Murdoch, Rupert	Novicki, Margaret A.	Packard, George R.
Murphy, Caryle Marie	Nuechterlein, Jeffrey D.	Paine, George C., II
Murphy, Joseph S.	Nugent, Walter	Pais, Abraham
Murphy, Richard W.	Nussbaum, Bruce	Pakula, Hannah C.
Murphy, Sean David	Nye, Joseph S., Jr.	Palmer, Norman D.
Murphy, Thomas S.		Palmer, Robbie Mark
Murray, Allen E.	**O**	Palmer, Ronald D.
Murray, Douglas P.	Oakes, John B.	Palmieri, Victor H.
Murray, Lori Esposito	Oakes, John G.H.	Panofsky, Wolfgang K.H.
Muse, Martha T.	Oakley, Phyllis E.	Parker, Barrington Daniels,
Muskie, Edmund S.	Oakley, Robert B.	Jr.
Myerson, Toby S.	Oberdorfer, Don	Parker, Jason H.
	O'Brien, Dennis J.	Parker, Maynard
N	O'Cleireacain, Carol	Parker, Richard B.
Nachmanoff, Arnold	O'Connell Mary Ellen	Parkinson, Roger
Nacht, Michael	O'Connor, Sandra Day	Parsky, Gerald L.
Nadiri, M. Ishaq	O'Connor, Walter F.	Parsons, Richard D.
Nagorski, Andrew	Odeen, Philip A.	Passer-Muslin, Juliette M.
Nagorski, Zygmunt	Odell, John S.	Passin, Herbert
Namkung, K. A.	Odom, William E.	Patrick, Hugh T.
Nathan, James A.	O'Donnell, Kevin	Patrikis, Ernest T.
Natt, Ted M.	Oettinger, Anthony G.	Patterson, Gardner
Nau, Henry R.	Offit, Morris W.	Patterson, Hugh B., Jr.
Navab, Alexander	O'Flaherty, J. Daniel	Paul, Roland A.
Naylor, Rosamond Lee	Ogden, Alfred	Payne, Donald M.
Negroponte, John D.	Ogden, William S.	Pearce, William R.
Neier, Aryeh	O'Hare, Joseph A.	Pearlstine, Norman
Nelson, Anne	Okawara, Merle Aiko	Pearson, John E.
Nelson, Daniel N.	Oksenberg, Michel	Pearson, Scott D.
Nelson, Jack	Okun, Herbert S.	Pedersen, Richard F.
Nelson, Merlin E.	Oliva, L. Jay	Pederson, Rena
Nenneman, Richard A.	Oliver, April	Pell, Claiborne
Neustadt, Richard E.	Oliver, Covey T.	Pelletreau, Robert H., Jr.
Newburg, Andre W.G.	Olmstead, Cecil J.	Pelson, Victor A.
Newell, Barbara W.	Olson, William C.	Penfield, James K.
Newhouse, John	Olvey, Lee D.	Percy, Charles H.
Newman, Priscilla A.	O'Malley, Cormac K.H.	Perella, Joseph Robert
Newman, Richard T.	Omestad, Thomas	Peretz, Don
Newsom, David D.	O'Neill, Michael J.	Perez, Antonio F.
Newton, Quigg	Opel, John R.	Perkin, Linda J.
Ney, Edward N.	Oppenheimer, Franz M.	Perkins, Edward J.
Nicholas, N. J., Jr.	Oppenheimer, Michael F.	Perkins, James A.
Nichols, Rodney W.	Orlins, Stephen A.	Perkins, Roswell B.
Niehuss, John M.	Ornstein, Norman J.	Perkovich, George
Niehuss, Rosemary Neaher	Osborne, Richard de J.	Perle, Richard N.
Nielsen, Waldemar A.	O'Shaughnessy, Elise	Perlman, Janice E.
Nierenberg, Claudia	Osmer-McQuade, Margaret	Perlmutter, Amos
Nilsson, A. Kenneth	Osnos, Peter	Perry, Robert C.
Nimetz, Matthew	Osnos, Susan Sherer	Peters, Arthur King
Nitze, Paul H.	Ostrander, F. Taylor	Peters, Aulana L.
Nitze, William A.	Overholser, Geneva	Petersen, Howard C.

Peterson, Erik R.	Posner, Michael H.	Ravitch, Richard
Peterson, Holly	Posvar, Wesley W.	Raymond, David A.
Peterson Peter G.	Potter, William C.	Raymond, Jack
Peterson, Rudolph A.	Powell, Colin L.	Raymond, Lee R.
Petree, Richard W.	Power, Philip H.	Reback, Sanford C.
Petree, Richard W., Jr.	Powers, Averill L.	Reed, Charles B.
Petri, Thomas E.	Powers, Thomas Moore	Reed, John S.
Petschek, Stephen R.	Pranger, Robert J.	Reed, Joseph Verner
Pettibone, Peter J.	Precht, Henry	Reeves, Jay B.L.
Petty, John R.	Press, Frank	Reichert, Douglas D.
Peyronnin, Joseph	Pressler, Larry	Reid, Ogden
Pezzullo, Lawrence A.	Preston, Lewis T.	Reid, Whitelaw
Pfaltzgraff, Robert L., Jr.	Prewitt, Kenneth	Reinhardt, John E.
Pfeiffer, Jane Cahill	Price, Daniel M.	Reinke, Fred W.
Pfeiffer, Ralph A., Jr.	Price, Hugh	Reisman, W. M.
Pfeiffer, Steven B.	Price, John R., Jr.	Reiss, Mitchell B.
Pham, Kien D.	Price, Robert	Renfrew, Charles B.
Pharr, Susan J.	Pritzker, Penny	Rennie, Renate
Phelan, John J., Jr.	Pryce, Jeffrey F.	Reppy, Judith V.
Phillips, Christopher H.	Puchala, Donald J.	Resor, Stanley R.
Phillips, Russell A., Jr.	Puckett, Allen E.	Rey, Nicholas A.
Picker, Harvey	Puckett, Robert H.	Reynolds, A. William
Pickering, Thomas R.	Purcell, Susan Kaufman	Rhinelander, John B.
Pieczenik, Steve R.	Pursley, Robert E.	Rhinesmith, Stephen H.
Piel, Gerard	Pusey, Nathan M.	Rhodes, Edward
Pierce, Ponchitta	Pustay, John S.	Rhodes, Frank H.T.
Pierre, Andrew J.	Putnam, Robert D.	Rhodes, John B., Sr.
Pifer, Alan	Pye, A. Kenneth	Rhodes, Thomas L.
Pigott, Charles M.	Pye, Lucian W.	Rhodes, William R.
Pike, John E.	Pyle, Cassandra A.	Ribicoff, Abraham A.
Pilling, Donald L.	Pyle, Kenneth B.	Rice, Condoleezza
Pilliod, Charles J., Jr.		Rice, Donald B.
Pincus, Lionel I.	**Q**	Rice, Donald S.
Pincus, Walter H.	Quandt, William B.	Rice, Joseph A.
Pinder, Jeanne	Quester, George H.	Rice, Susan E.
Pinkerton, W. Stewart	Quigley, Kevin F.F.	Rich, John H., Jr.
Pino, John A.	Quigley, Leonard V.	Rich, Michael D.
Pipes, Daniel	Quinn, Jane Bryant	Richards, Paul G.
Pipes, Richard E.		Richardson, David B.
Pisano, Jane G.	**R**	Richardson, Elliot L.
Platt, Alan A.	Rabb, Maxwell M.	Richardson, Henry J., III
Platt, Alexander Hartley	Rabinowitch, Alexander	Richardson, John
Platt, Nicholas	Rabinowitch, Victor	Richardson, Richard W.
Plimpton, Calvin H.	Rademaker, Stephen G.	Richardson, William B.
Ploumpis, Valerie	Radway, Laurence I.	Richardson, William R.
Poats, Rutherford M.	Ragone, David V.	Richardson, Yolonda
Pocalyko, Michael N.	Raines, Franklin D.	Richman, Joan F.
Podhoretz, Norman	Raisian, John	Richter, Anthony H.
Pogue, Richard W.	Ralph, Regan Elisabeth	Ridgway, Rozanne L.
Polk, William R.	Ramirez, Lilia L.	Rielly, John E.
Pollack, Gerald A.	Ramo, Simon	Ries, Hans A.
Pollack, Lester	Ranis, Gustav	Riesel, Victor
Polsby, Nelson W.	Rashish, Myer	Riley, Kevin Jack
Pond, Elizabeth	Ratchford, J. Thomas	Rindskopf, Elizabeth R.
Poneman, Daniel B.	Rather, Dan	Riordan, Michael L.
Pool, Marquita J.	Rathjens, George W.	Ritch, John B., III
Pope, Clara A.	Ratner, Steven R.	Rivers, Richard R.
Popoff, Frank P.	Rattner, Steven L.	Rivkin, Donald H.
Portes, Richard D.	Rauch, Rudolph S.	Rivlin, Alice M.
Porzecanski, Arturo C.	Ravenal, Earl C.	Rizopoulos, Nicholas X.
Posen, Barry R.	Ravenholt, Albert	Robb, Charles S.

Robbins, Carla Anne
Robert, Stephen
Roberts, Chalmers M.
Roberts, John J.
Roberts, Walter R.
Robinson, David Z.
Robinson, Davis R.
Robinson, Elizabeth L.
Robinson, James D., III
Robinson, Leonard H., Jr.
Robinson, Linda S.
Robinson, Marshall A.
Robinson, Pearl T.
Robinson, Randall
Robison, Olin C.
Roche, James G.
Rocke, Mark D.
Rockefeller, David
Rockefeller, David, Jr.
Rockefeller, John D., IV
Rockefeller, Nicholas
Rockefeller, Rodman C.
Rockwell, Hays H.
Rodman, Peter W.
Rodriguez, Rita M.
Rodriguez, Vincent A.
Roett, Riordan
Roff, J. Hugh, Jr.
Rogers, Bernard W.
Rogers, William D.
Rogers, William P.
Rogovin, Mitchell
Rohatyn, Felix G.
Rohlen, Thomas P.
Rokke, Ervin J.
Romberg, Alan D.
Romero, Philip J.
Romero-Barcelo, Carlos
Roney, John H.
Roosevelt, Theodore, IV
Rosberg, Carl G.
Rose, Daniel
Rose, Elihu
Rose, Frederick P.
Rosecrance, Richard
Rosen, Arthur H.
Rosen, Jane K.
Rosenberg, Tina
Rosenblatt, Lionel
Rosenblatt, Peter R.
Rosenblum, Mort
Rosenfeld, Stephen S.
Rosenfield, Patricia L.
Rosenstock, Robert
Rosenthal, A. M.
Rosenthal, Douglas E.
Rosenthal, Jack
Rosenthal, Joel H.
Rosenzweig, Robert M.
Rosin, Axel G.
Roskens, Ronald W.

Rosovsky, Henry
Ross, Alison K.
Ross, Arthur
Ross, Dennis B.
Ross, James D.
Ross, Roger
Ross, Thomas B.
Rosso, David J.
Rossotti, Charles O.
Rostow, Elspeth Davies
Rostow, Eugene V.
Rostow, Nicholas
Rostow, Walt W.
Rotberg, Robert I.
Roth, Kenneth
Roth, William M.
Roth, William V., Jr.
Rothkopf, David J.
Rovine, Arthur W.
Rowen, Henry S.
Rowen, Hobart
Rowny, Edward L.
Rubin, Barnett R.
Rubin, James P.
Rubin, Nancy H.
Rubin, Robert E.
Rubin, Seymour J.
Rubin, Trudy
Ruckelshaus, William D.
Rudenstine, Neil L.
Rudman, Warren B.
Rudolph, Barbara
Rudolph, Lloyd I.
Rudolph, Susanne Hoeber
Ruebhausen, Oscar M.
Ruenitz, Robert M.
Ruggie, John G.
Runge, C. Ford
Russell, Thomas W., Jr.
Rustow, Dankwart A.
Ruttan, Vernon W.
Ryan, Arthur F.
Ryan, John T., Jr.
Ryan, John T., III

S

Sachs, Jeffrey D.
Sacks, Paul M.
Safran, Nadav
Sagan, Carl E.
Sagan, Scott D.
Said, Edward
Sakoian, Carol Knuth
Salacuse, Jeswald W.
Salerno, Frederic V.
Salk, Jonas
Salomon, Richard E.
Salomon, William R.
Sample, Steven B.
Samuels, Barbara C., II
Samuels, Michael A.

Samuels, Nathaniel
Samuels, Richard J.
Sanchez, Miguel A.
Sanchez, Nestor D.
Sander, Alison
Sanders, Edward G.
Sanders, J. Stanley
Sanford, Charles S., Jr.
Sanford, Terry
Santos, Charles
Sapiro, Miriam
Sapolsky, Harvey M.
Sato, Kumi
Saul, Ralph S.
Saunders, Harold H.
Savage, Frank
Sawhill, John C.
Sawyer, David H.
Sawyer, Diane
Sawyer, John E.
Scalapino, Robert A.
Scali, John A.
Schacht, Henry B.
Schachter, Oscar
Schaetzel, J. Robert
Schaffer, Howard B.
Schake, Kori
Schaufele, William E., Jr.
Schecter, Jerrold
Scheffer, David J.
Scheinman, Lawrence
Schell, Orville H.
Schick, Thomas
Schiff, Frank W.
Schifter, Richard
Schilling, Warner R.
Schlesinger, Arthur, Jr.
Schlesinger, James R.
Schlesinger, Stephen, Jr.
Schlosser, Herbert S.
Schmertz, Herbert
Schmidt, Benno, Jr.
Schmoke, Kurt L.
Schneider, Jan
Schneider, William
Schneier, Arthur
Schoettle, Enid C.B.
Schorr, Daniel L.
Schrage, Elliot J.
Schroeder, Patricia
Schubert, Richard F.
Schuh, G. Edward
Schulhof, Michael P.
Schwab, Susan C.
Schwab, William B.
Schwartz, Eric Paul
Schwarz, Frederick A. O., Jr.
Schwarzer, William W.
Schwarzman, Stephen A.
Schwebel, Stephen M.
Sciolino, Elaine F.

Scowcroft, Brent
Scranton, William W.
Seaborg, Glenn T.
Seagrave, Norman P.
Seamans, Robert C., Jr.
Segal, Sheldon J.
Segal, Susan L.
Seib, Gerald
Seibold, Frederick C., Jr.
Seidman, Herta Lande
Seigenthaler, John L.
Seitz, Frederick
Sekulow, Eugene A.
Selin, Ivan
Semple, Robert B., Jr.
Sewall, John O.B.
Sewall, Sarah Bulkeley
Sewell, John W.
Seymour, Frances J.
Shafer, D. Michael
Shaffer, Gail S.
Shalala, Donna E.
Shapiro, Eli
Shapiro, Harold T.
Shapiro, Isaac
Sharp, Daniel A.
Shayne, Herbert M.
Sheeline, Paul C.
Sheffield, James R.
Sheffield, Jill W.
Sheinbaum, Stanley K.
Sheinkman, Jack
Sheldon, Eleanor Bernert
Shelley, Sally Swing
Shelp, Ronald K.
Shelton, Joanna Reed
Shelton, Sally A.
Shenk, George H.
Sherry, George L.
Sherwood, Ben
Sherwood, Elizabeth D.
Shestack, Jerome J.
Shiner, Josette
Shipley, Walter V.
Shirk, Susan L.
Shlaes, Amity
Shoemaker, Alvin V.
Shoemaker, Christopher Cole
Shoemaker, Don
Shriver, Donald W., Jr.
Shriver, Sargent, Jr.
Shubert, Gustave H.
Shulman, Colette
Shulman, Marshall D.
Shultz, George P.
Sick, Gary G.
Siegman, Henry
Sifton, Elisabeth
Sigal, Leon V.
Sigmund, Paul E.

Silas, C. J.
Silberman, Laurence H.
Silk, Leonard S.
Silkenat, James R.
Silver, Daniel B.
Silver, Ron
Silvers, Robert B.
Simes, Dimitri K.
Simmons, Adele Smith
Simon, William E.
Sims, Albert G.
Sinclair, Paula
Sinding, Steven W.
Sinkin, Richard N.
Sisco, Joseph J.
Sitrick, James B.
Skidmore, Thomas E.
Skinner, Elliott P.
Skolnikoff, Eugene B.
Slater, Joseph E.
Slawson, Paul S.
Sloane, Ann Brownell
Slocombe, Walter B.
Sloss, Leon
Small, Lawrence M.
Smalley, Patricia T.
Smart, S. Bruce, Jr.
Smith, Andrew F.
Smith, Clint E.
Smith, David S.
Smith, DeWitt C., Jr.
Smith, Edwin M.
Smith, Gaddis
Smith, Gare A.
Smith, Hedrick L.
Smith, Jeffrey H.
Smith, John T., II
Smith, Larry
Smith, Leighton W., Jr.
Smith, Malcolm B.
Smith, Michael B.
Smith, Perry M.
Smith, Peter B.
Smith, Peter Hopkinson
Smith, R. Jeffrey
Smith, Richard M.
Smith, Stephen G.
Smith, Theodore M.
Smith, Tony
Smith, W. Y.
Smith, Wayne S.
Smith, Winthrop H., Jr.
Smythe, Mabel M.
Snow, Robert Anthony
Snowe, Olympia J.
Snyder, David M.
Snyder, Jack L.
Snyder, Jed C.
Snyder, Richard E.
Sobol, Dorothy Meadow
Soderberg, Nancy E.

Sofaer, Abraham David
Sohn, Louis B.
Solarz, Stephen J.
Solbert, Peter O.A.
Solnick, Steven L.
Solomon, Anne G.K.
Solomon, Anthony M.
Solomon, Peter J.
Solomon, Richard H.
Solomon, Robert
Sonenshine, H. Marshall
Sonenshine, Tara
Sonne, Christian R.
Sonnenberg, Maurice
Sonnenfeldt, Helmut
Sonnenfeldt, Richard W.
Sorensen, Gillian Martin
Sorensen, Theodore C.
Soros, George
Soros, Paul
Sovern, Michael I.
Spain, James W.
Spalter, Jonathan
Spar, Debora L.
Spector, Leonard S.
Speidel, Kirsten Elizabeth
Spencer, Edson W.
Spencer, John H.
Spencer, William C.
Spero, Joan E.
Speth, James Gustave
Speyer, Jerry I.
Spielvogel, Carl
Spiers, Ronald I.
Spiro, Herbert J.
Spiro, Peter J.
Spratt, John M., Jr.
Squadron, Howard M.
Stacks, John
Staheli, Donald L.
Stalson, Helena
Stamas, Stephen
Stankard, Francis X.
Stanley, Peter W.
Stanley, Timothy W.
Stanton, Frank
Stanton, R. John, Jr.
Staples, Eugene S.
Starobin, Herman
Starr, John Bryan
Starr, S. Frederick
Stassen, Harold E.
Steadman, Richard C.
Steel, Ronald
Stegemeier, Richard J.
Steiger, Paul E.
Stein, David Fred
Stein, Elliot, Jr.
Stein, Eric
Steinberg, David J.
Steinberg, James B.

Steinbruner, John D.	Summers, Harry G., Jr.	Thurman, M. R.
Steiner, Daniel	Summers, Lawrence H.	Tierney, Paul E., Jr.
Steiner, Joshua L.	Sunderland, Jack B.	Tigert, Ricki Rhodarmer
Stent, Angela E.	Suslow, Leo A.	Tillinghast, David R.
Stepan, Alfred C.	Sutterlin, James S.	Tillman, Seth P.
Stephanopoulos, George R.	Sutton, Francis X.	Timothy, Kristen
Stern, Ernest	Swank, Emory C.	Timpson, Sarah L.
Stern, Fritz	Swanson, David H.	Tipson, Frederick S.
Stern, H. Peter	Sweitzer, Brandon W.	Tisch, Laurence A.
Stern, Paula	Swenson, Eric P.	Tobias, Randall L.
Stern, Walter P.	Swid, Stephen C.	Todaro, Michael P.
Sterner, Michael E.	Swiers, Peter Bird	Todd, Maurice Linwood
Sternlight, David	Swing, John Temple	Todman, Terence A.
Stevens, Charles R.	Szanton, Peter L.	Toll, Maynard J., Jr.
Stevens, James W.	Szporluk, Roman	Tomlinson, Alexander C.
Stevens, Norton		Topping, Seymour
Stevens, Paul Schott	**T**	Torres, Art
Stevenson, Adlai E., III	Taft, Julia V.	Torres, Raidza M.
Stevenson, Charles A.	Taft, William H., IV	Torricelli, Robert G.
Stevenson, John R.	Tagliabue, Paul	Toth, Robert C.
Stewart, Donald M.	Tahir-Kheli, Shirin R.	Townley, Preston
Stewart, Gordon C.	Talbot, Phillips	Trachtenberg, Stephen Joel
Stewart, Patricia Carry	Talbott, Strobe	Train, Harry D., II
Stewart, Ruth Ann	Tang, David K.Y.	Train, John
Stiehm, Judith Hicks	Tanham, George K.	Train, Russell E.
Stifel, Laurence D.	Tannenwald, Theodore, Jr.	Trainor, Bernard E.
Stith, Kate	Tanner, Harold	Trani, Eugene P.
Stobaugh, Robert B.	Tanter, Raymond	Travis, Martin B., Jr.
Stockman, David A.	Tapia, Raul R.	Treat, John Elting
Stoessinger, John G.	Tarnoff, Peter	Trebat, Thomas J.
Stofft, William A.	Tasco, Frank J.	Treverton, Gregory F.
Stoga, Alan	Taubman, William	Trezise, Philip H.
Stokes, Bruce	Taylor, Arthur R.	Trooboff, Peter D.
Stokes, Donald E.	Taylor, Kathryn Pelgrift	Trowbridge, Alexander B.
Stokes, Louis	Taylor, Milbrey Rennie	Truman, Edwin M.
Stone, Jeremy J.	Taylor, William J., Jr.	Tsipis, Kosta
Stone, Michael P.W.	Tedstrom, John E.	Tucher, H. Anton
Stone, Roger D.	Teece, David J.	Tuck, Edward Hallam
Straus, Donald B.	Teeley, Peter B.	Tucker, Nancy Bernkopf
Straus, Oscar S., II	Teeters, Nancy H.	Tucker, Richard F.
Straus, R. Peter	Teitelbaum, Michael S.	Tucker, Robert W.
Strauss, Robert S.	Telhami, Shibley	Tung, Ko-Yung
Strauss, Simon D.	Tempelsman, Maurice	Turck, Nancy B.
Strausz-Hupe, Robert	Tennyson, Leonard B.	Turkevich, John
Stremlau, John J.	Terracciano, Anthony P.	Turner, J. Michael
Strock, James M.	Terry, Sarah M.	Turner, Robert F.
Stromseth, Jane E.	Thayer, A. Bronson	Turner, Stansfield
Stroock, Thomas F.	Theobald, Thomas C.	Turner, William C.
Strossen, Nadine	Thoman, G. Richard	Tuthill, John Wills
Stroud, Joe H.	Thomas, Barbara S.	Tyrrell, R. Emmett, Jr.
Studeman, William O.	Thomas, Brooks	Tyson, Laura D'Andrea
Styron, Rose	Thomas, Evan W., III	
Sudarkasa, Michael E.M.	Thomas, Franklin A.	**U**
Sudarkasa, Niara	Thomas, Lee B., Jr.	Udovitch, A. L.
Sughrue, Karen M.	Thompson, W. Scott	Uhlig, Mark
Suleiman, Ezra N.	Thomson, James A.	Ullman, Richard H.
Sullivan, Gordon Russell	Thomson, James C., Jr.	Ulman, Cornelius M.
Sullivan, Leon H.	Thornburgh, Dick	Ulrich, Marybeth Peterson
Sullivan, Margaret C.	Thornell, Richard P.	Ungar, Sanford J.
Sullivan, Roger W.	Thornton, Thomas P.	Unger, David
Sullivan, William H.	Thoron, Louisa	Unger, Leonard

Upton, Maureen	Wahl, Nicholas	Welch, C. David
Uriu, Robert	Wais, Marshall Ivan, Jr.	Welch, Jasper A., Jr.
Usher, William R.	Wakeman, Frederic E., Jr.	Welch, John F., Jr.
Utgoff, Victor A.	Wales, Jane	Welch, Larry D.
Utley, Garrick	Walker, Charls E.	Weller, Ralph A.
Utton, Albert E.	Walker, G. R.	Wells, Damon, Jr.
	Walker, Jenonne	Wells, Herman B.

V

	Walker, John L.	Wells, Louis T., Jr.
Vagliano, Alexander M.	Walker, Mary Lynn	Wells, Samuel F., Jr.
Vagliano, Sara	Walker, Nancy J.	Wender, Ira T.
Vaky, Viron P.	Walker, William N.	Wendt, E. Allan
Valdez, Abelardo Lopez	Wallander, Celeste A.	Wertheim, Mitzi M.
Valenta, Jiri	Wallerstein, Mitchel B.	Wesely, Edwin J.
Valentine, Debra A.	Wallison, Peter J.	Wessel, Michael R.
Valenzuela, Arturo	Walsh, Michaela	West, J. Robinson
Vance, Cyrus R.	Walters, Barbara	Weston, Burns H.
Vande Berg, Marsha	Walton, Anthony J.	Wexler, Anne
VanDeMark, Brian	Waltz, Kenneth N.	Weymouth, Lally G.
vanden Heuvel, Katrina	Ward, John W.	Whalen, Charles W., Jr.
vanden Heuvel, William J.	Ward, Katherine T.	Whalen, Richard J.
Van Dusen, Michael H.	Ward, Patrick Joseph	Wharton, Clifton R., Jr.
Van Dyk, Ted	Ware, Carl	Wheat, Francis M.
Van Evera, Stephen W.	Warner, Edward L., III	Wheeler, John K.
Van Fleet, James A.	Warner, Volney J.	Whitaker, C. S.
Van Vlierden, Constant M.	Warnke, Paul C.	Whitaker, Jennifer Seymour
Van Voorst, L. Bruce	Warren, Gerald L.	Whitaker, Mark
Veblen, Tom C.	Washburn, Abbott M.	White, John P.
Vecchio, Mark S.	Washburn, John L.	White, Julia A.
Veit, Carol M.	Wasserstein, Bruce	White, Peter C.
Veit, Lawrence A.	Waterbury, John	White, Robert J.
Veliotes, Nicholas A.	Waters, Cherri D.	White, Robert M.
Vermilye, Peter H.	Watson, Alexander F.	White, Walter H., Jr.
Vernon, Raymond	Wattenberg, Ben J.	Whitehead, John C.
Verville, Elizabeth G.	Watts, Glenn E.	Whitehouse, Charles S.
Vessey, John W.	Watts, John H.	Whitman, Marina v.N.
Vest, George S.	Watts, William	Whitney, Craig R.
Viccellio, Henry, Jr.	Way, Alva O.	Whittemore, Frederick B.
Viederman, Stephen	Weatherstone, Dennis	Whyman, William
Viets, Richard Noyes	Weaver, David R.	Wiarda, Howard J.
Vila, Adis Maria	Weaver, George L-P	Widner, Jennifer
Villar, Arturo	Webster, William H.	Wiener, Carolyn Seely
Vine, Richard D.	Wedgwood, Ruth	Wiener, Malcolm H.
Viorst, Milton	Wehrle, Leroy S.	Wiesel, Elie
Viscusi, Enzo	Weidenbaum, Murray L.	Wiesel, Torsten
Vitale, Alberto	Weigel, George	Wieseltier, Leon
Voell, Richard A.	Weiksner, George B., Jr.	Wiesner, Jerome B.
Vogel, Ezra F.	Weil, Frank A.	Wildenthal, C. Kern
Vogelgesang, Sandy	Weinberg, John L.	Wilds, Walter
Vojta, George J.	Weinberg, Steven	Wiley, Richard A.
Volcker, Paul A.	Weinberger, Caspar W.	Wiley, W. Bradford
Volk, Stephen R.	Weiner, Myron	Wilhelm, Harry E.
Von Klemperer, Alfred H.	Weinert, Richard S.	Wilhelm, Robert E.
Von Mehren, Robert B.	Weinrod, W. Bruce	Wilkie, Edith B.
Votaw, Carmen Delgado	Weinstein, Michael M.	Wilkins, Roger W.
Vuono, Carl E.	Weintraub, Sidney	Wilkinson, Sharon
	Weisman, Steven	Williams, Aaron S.

W

	Weiss, Charles, Jr.	Williams, Avon N., III
Wachner, Linda Joy	Weiss, Cora	Williams, Earle C.
Waddell, Rick	Weiss, Edith Brown	Williams, Eddie Nathan
Wadsworth-Darby, Mary	Weiss, Thomas G.	Williams, H. Roy
Waggoner, Robert C.	Weitz, Peter R.	Williams, Harold M.

Williams, Haydn
Williams, Joseph H.
Williams, Maurice J.
Williams, Reba White
Williamson, Irving A.
Williamson, Thomas S., Jr.
Willrich, Mason
Wilmers, Robert G.
Wilson, Donald M.
Wilson, Ernest James, III
Wilson, John D.
Wimpfheimer, Jacques D.
Wing, Adrien Katherine
Winner, Andrew C.
Winokur, Herbert S., Jr.
Winship, Thomas
Winston, Michael R.
Winterer, Philip S.
Winters, Francis X.
Wirth, John D.
Wirth, Timothy E.
Wisner, Frank G., II
Wisner, Graham G.
Witunski, Michael
Woerner, Fred F.
Wofford, Harris L.
Wohl, Richard H.
Wohlforth, William C.
Wohlstetter, Albert
Wohlstetter, Roberta
Wolf, Charles, Jr.
Wolf, Milton A.
Wolfensohn, James D.

Wolff, Alan Wm.
Wolfowitz, Paul D.
Wolin, Neal S.
Wolpe, Howard
Wood, Joseph R.
Woodward, Susan L.
Woolf, Harry
Woolsey, R. James
Wray, Cecil, Jr.
Wriggins, W. Howard
Wright, Robin
Wright-Carozza, Paolo G.
Wyman, Thomas H.

Y

Yacoubian, Mona
Yalman, Nur
Yang, James Ting-Yeh
Yankelovich, Daniel
Yarmolinsky, Adam
Yergin, Daniel H.
Yochelson, John N.
Yoffie, David B.
Yoshihara, Nancy Akemi
Yost, Casimir A.
Young, Alice
Young, Andrew
Young, Edgar B.
Young, George H., III
Young, Joan P.
Young, M. Crawford
Young, Nancy
Young, Peter Joel C.

Young, Stephen B.
Youngman, William S.
Yu, Frederick T.C.
Yudkin, Richard A.

Z

Zagoria, Donald S.
Zakheim, Dov S.
Zarb, Frank G.
Zartman, I. William
Zeidenstein, George
Zelikow, Philip D.
Zelnick, C. Robert
Zemmol, Jonathan I.
Zilkha, Ezra K.
Zimmerman, Edwin M.
Zimmerman, Peter D.
Zimmerman, William
Zimmermann, Warren
Zinberg, Dorothy S.
Zinder, Norton D.
Zoellick, Robert B.
Zogby, James J.
Zolberg, Aristide R.
Zonis, Marvin
Zorthian, Barry
Zraket, Charles A.
Zuckerman, Harriet
Zuckerman, Mortimer B.
Zumwalt, Elmo R., Jr.
Zwick, Charles J.
Zysman, John

The Council on Foreign Relations is located at
58 East 68th Street, New York, NY, 10021.

Appendix B

THE TRILATERAL COMMISSION
Membership Roster, March 1994

Board Members

Otto Graf Lambsdorff
European Chairman

Akio Morita
Japanese Chairman

Garret FitzGerald
European
Deputy Chairman

Shijuro Ogata
Japanese
Deputy Chairman

Paul Révay
European Director

Tadashi Yamamoto
Japanese Director

Paul A. Volcker
North American Chairman

Allan E. Gotlieb
North American
Deputy Chairman

Charles B. Heck
North American Director

David Rockefeller
Founder and Honorary Chairman

Executive Committee

C. Fred Bergsten
Zbigniew Brzezinski
William T. Coleman, Jr.
Jessica P. Einhorn
L. Yves Fortier
Allan E. Gotlieb

Robert D. Haas
Henry A. Kissinger
Robert S. McNamara
David Rockefeller
Henry Rosovsky
Paul A. Volcker

North American Members

Paul A. Allaire, Chairman and Chief Executive Officer, Xerox Corporation

Dwayne O. Andreas, Chairman of the Board and Chief Executive Officer, Archer Daniels Midland Company

Rand V. Araskog, Chairman, President and Chief Executive Officer, ITT Corporation

C. Fred Bergsten, Director, Institute for International Economics; former U.S. Assistant Secretary of the Treasury for International Affairs

Conrad M. Black, Chairman and Chief Executive Officer, Hollinger Inc., Toronto

Stephen W. Bosworth, President, United States-Japan Foundation

Jacques Bougie, President and Chief Executive Officer, Alcan Aluminium, Ltd., Montreal

John Brademas, President Emeritus, New York University; former Member of U.S. House of Representatives

Harold Brown, Counselor, Center for Strategic and International Studies; former U.S. Secretary of Defense

Zbigniew Brzezinski, Counselor, Center for Strategic and International Studies; Robert Osgood Professor of American Foreign Affairs, Paul Nitze School of Advanced International Studies, Johns Hopkins University; former U.S. Assistant to the President for National Security Affairs

M. Anthony Burns, Chairman, President and Chief Executive Officer, Ryder System, Inc.

D. Wayne Calloway, Chairman and Chief Executive Officer, PepsiCo

Frank C. Carlucci, Vice Chairman, The Carlyle Group; former U.S. Secretary of Defense

John H. Chafee, Member of United States Senate

Marshall A. Cohen, President and Chief Executive Officer, The Molson Companies Ltd., Toronto

William S. Cohen, Member of United States Senate

William T. Coleman, Jr., Senior Partner, O'Melveny &

Thomas S. Foley, Former Speaker of the U.S. House of Representatives

L. Yves Fortier, Senior Partner, Ogilvy Renault, Barristers and Solicitors, Montreal; former Canadian Ambassador and Permanent Representative to the United Nations

Paolo Fresco, Vice Chairman of the Board and Executive Officer, The General Electric Company (U.S.A.)

Stephen Friedman, Senior Partner and Co-Chairman, Goldman, Sachs & Co.

Leslie H. Gelb, President, Council on Foreign Relations

John A. Georges, Chairman and Chief Executive Officer, International Paper

Neil Goldschmidt, Former Governor of Oregon; former U.S. Secretary of Transporation

Joseph T. Gorman, Chairman and Chief Executive Officer, TRW Inc.

Allan E. Gotlieb, Chairman, Canada Council; Chairman, Burson-Marsteller, Toronto; former Canadian Ambassador to the United States

Katharine Graham, Chairman of the Executive Committee, The Washington Post Company

William Graham, Member of the Canadian House of Commons and Vice Chairman of the Standing Committee on Foreign Affairs and International Trade

Maurice R. Greenberg, Chairman and Chief Executive Officer, American International Group, Inc.

John H. Gutfreund, Former Chairman of the Board and Chief Executive Officer, Salomon Inc.

Robert D. Haas, Chairman and Chief Executive Officer, Levi Strauss & Co.

Lee H. Hamilton, Member of U.S. House of Representatives

David J. Hennigar, Chairman, Crownx, Inc.; Vice-Chairman, Crown Life Insurance Company; Atlantic Regional Director, Burns Fry Limited, Halifax, Nova Scotia

Carla A. Hills, Chairman, Hills & Company; former U.S. Trade Representative

Robert D. Hormats, Vice Chairman, Goldman Sachs

International; former U.S. Assistant Secretary of State for Economic and Business Affairs

James R. Houghton, Chairman of the Board and Chief Executive Officer, Corning, Incorporated

Samuel C. Johnson, Chairman and Chief Executive Officer, S. C. Johnson & Son, Inc.

W. Thomas Johnson, President, Cable News Network

Vernon C. Jordan, Partner, Akin, Gump, Strauss, Hauer & Feld

Nannerl O. Keohane, President, Duke University

Donald R. Keough, Chairman of the Board, Allen & Company Incorporated; former President and Chief Operating Officer, The Coca-Cola Company

Henry A. Kissinger, Chairman, Kissinger Associates, Inc.; former U.S. Secretary of State; former U.S. Assistant to the President for National Security Affairs

Thomas G. Labrecque, Chairman and Chief Executive Officer, The Chase Manhattan Bank, N.A.

Jim Leach, Member of U.S. House of Representatives

Gerald Levin, Chairman and Chief Executive Officer, Time Warner

Whitney MacMillan, Chairman of the Board and Chief Executive Officer, Cargill, Inc.

Jay Mazur, President, International Ladies' Garment Workers Union

Hugh L. McColl, Jr., Chairman, President and Chief Executive Officer, NationsBank Corporation

Robert S. McNamara, Former President, The World Bank; former U.S. Secretary of Defense

Allen E. Murray, Former Chairman of the Board, President and Chief Executive Officer, Mobil Corporation

Michel Oksenberg, President, East-West Center, Hawaii

Henry Owen, Senior Fellow on leave, Brookings Institution; Member, Consultants International Group; former U.S. Ambassador-at-Large and Special Representative of the President for Economic Summits

James A. Pattison, Chairman, President and Chief Executive Officer, Jim Pattison Group Inc., Vancouver

Robert D. Putnam, Director of the Center for International Affairs and Clarence Dillon Professor of International Affairs, Harvard University

Charles B. Rangel, Member of U.S. House of Representatives

Lee R. Raymond, Chairman and Chief Executive Officer, Exxon Corporation

Rozanne Ridgway, Co-chair, Atlantic Council; former U.S. Assistant Secretary of State for European and Canadian Affairs

Charles S. Robb, Member of United States Senate; former Governor of Virginia

David Rockefeller, Founder and Honorary Chairman, Trilateral Commission

John D. Rockefeller IV, Member of United States Senate; former Governor of West Virginia

Henry Rosovsky, Lewis P. & Linda L. Geyser University Professor, Harvard University

William V. Roth, Jr., Member of United States Senate

William D. Ruckelshaus, Chairman and Chief Executive Officer, Browning-Ferris Industries; former Administrator, U.S. Environmental Protection Agency; former U.S. Deputy Attorney General

Kurt L. Schmoke, Mayor of Baltimore

Albert Shanker, President, American Federation of Teachers

Walter V. Shipley, Chairman and Chief Operating Officer, Chemical Banking Corporation

George P. Shultz, Honorary Fellow, Hoover Institution, Stanford University; former U.S. Secretary of State; former U.S. Secretary of the Treasury; former U.S. Secretary of Labor; former Director, U.S. Office of Management and Budget

C. J. Silas, Chairman of the Board and Chief Executive Officer, Phillips Petroleum Company

Gerard C. Smith, Former Head of U.S. Arms Control and Disarmament Agency and Chief Negotiator of SALT I; former Ambassador-at-Large for Non-Proliferation Matters

Ronald D. Southern, Chairman, President and Chief

Executive Officer, ATCO Ltd., Calgary; Chairman, Canadian Utilities Ltd., Edmonton

Paula Stern, Senior Fellow, The Progressive Policy Institute, Washington, D.C.; President, The Stern Group; former Chairwoman, U.S. International Trade Commission

Wilson H. Taylor, Chairman, President and Chief Executive Officer, CIGNA Corporation

William I.M. Turner, Jr., Chairman and Chief Executive Officer, Exsultate, Inc., Montreal

Ko-Yung Tung, Chairman, Global Practice Group, O'Melveny & Myers, New York

Paul A. Volcker, Chairman, James D. Wolfensohn Inc., New York; Frederick H. Schultz Professor of International Economic Policy, Princeton University; former Chairman, Board of Governors, U.S. Federal Reserve System

Glenn E. Watts, President Emeritus, Communications Workers of America

Henry Wendt, Chairman, SmithKlineBeecham

Marina v.N. Whitman, Distinguished Visiting Professor of Business Administration and Public Policy, The University of Michigan

Robert N. Wilson, Vice Chairman, Johnson & Johnson

Robert C. Winters, Chairman, President and Chief Executive Officer, Prudential Insurance Co. of America

Robert B. Zoellick, Executive Vice-President, General Counsel and Secretary, Federal National Mortgage Association; former Under Secretary of State for Economic Affairs

Former Members in Public Service

Bruce Babbitt, U.S. Secretary of the Interior

Warren Christopher, U.S. Secretary of State

Henry Cisneros, U.S. Secretary of Housing and Urban Development

Bill Clinton, President of the United States

Lynn E. Davis, U.S. Under Secretary of State for

International Security Affairs
John M. Deutch, U.S. Under Secretary of Defense for Acquisition and Technology
David Gergen, U.S. Assistant to the President for Communications
Richard N. Gardner, U.S. Ambassador to Spain
Alan Greenspan, Chairman, Board of Governors, U.S. Federal Reserve System
Richard Holbrooke, U.S. Ambassador to Germany
James R. Jones, U.S. Ambassador to Mexico
Winston Lord, U.S. Assistant Secretary of State for East Asian and Pacific Affairs
Walter F. Mondale, U.S. Ambassador to Japan
Roy MacLaren, Canadian Minister of International Trade
Joseph S. Nye, Jr., Chairman, National Intelligence Council, Central Intelligence Agency
Alice M. Rivlin, Deputy Director, U.S. Office of Management and Budget
Donna E. Shalala, U.S. Secretary of Health and Human Services
Joan Edelman Spero, U.S. Under Secretary of State for Economic and Agricultural Affairs

---

Japanese and European Members are not listed here.

The Trilateral Commission headquarters is located at 345 East 46th Street, New York, NY 10017.

Wake the Town and Tell the People!

Millions of Americans have become disturbed about the leadership our nation continues to endure. Even more are concerned about the future for themselves and their children.

You can help fellow Americans understand the source of their worries, and also what to do about getting America back on track.

Order additional copies of *The Insiders* now.

- For friends, neighbors and acquaintances.
- For anyone involved in political activity.
- For students and teachers.
- For businessmen, doctors, accountants, lawyers, and taxpayers.
- For press, radio and television reporters and executives.
- For anyone who wants to know what the "new world order" means for America, and how to keep our nation from its clutches.

1–9 copies.. $3.00 each*
10–49 copies .... $2.50 each*
50 copies (case lot).................................. $100.00**

* Please add 15 percent ($2.00 minimum) for postage and handling.
** No postage and handling charge for case lot orders.

The John Birch Society
P.O. Box 8040
Appleton, WI 54913

(Credit card orders accepted at 414–749–3783.)

RECOMMENDED READING

The Shadows of Power **$10.95**
 JAMES PERLOFF — The history of the Council on Foreign Relations compiled from the group's own documents. 1988 pb

Financial Terrorism **$8.95**
 JOHN F. MCMANUS — The Insiders' plan to hijack America through debt, inflation, entitlements, and the Fed. 1993 pb

The Blue Book of the John Birch Society **$4.00**
 ROBERT WELCH — The unabridged transcript of the two-day presentation that launched this organization in 1958. pb

The Fearful Master **$4.95**
 G. EDWARD GRIFFIN — An early criticism of the United Nations, including the backgrounds of its founders and their intentions. 1964 pb

Global Tyranny ... Step By Step **$12.95**
 WILLIAM F. JASPER — The UN must be stopped or it will rule the world in a tyrannical new world order. 1992 pb

John Birch Society Introductory Packet **$5.00**
 Numerous pamphlets analyzing current events, a sample *JBS Bulletin*, and a sample of *The New American* magazine.

Especially Recommended

The New American .... **(see below)**
 The New American magazine, a biweekly publication affiliated with The John Birch Society, is must reading for those who would be truly informed about the plans and programs of the Insiders.

 • **Six months subscription** **$22.00**
 • **One year subscription** **$39.00**

Please contact *The New American* for foreign rates.

Except for subscriptions to *The New American*, please add 15 percent for postage and handling. ($2.00 minimum)

The John Birch Society
P.O. Box 8040
Appleton, WI 54913

(Credit card orders accepted at 414–749–3783.)